Guitar

MILOŠ KARADAGLIĆ
WITH CARL HERRING

PLAY GUITAR WITH MILOŠ
LEVEL 1

Learn the secrets of the world's most loved classical guitarist

www.playguitarwithmilos.com

ED 13931
ISBN 978-1-8476-1490-2
ISMN 979-0-2201-3750-1

www.schott-music.com

Mainz • London • Madrid • Berlin • New York • Paris • Prague • Tokyo • Toronto
© 2018 SCHOTT MUSIC Ltd, London

ED 13931
ISBN 978-1-8476-1490-2
ISMN 979-0-2201-3750-1

Editor: Tony Mizen

Cover Photograph: James Cheadle
Backcover and inside photography: Mélanie Gomez Photography, Mainz
Other photographs:
White Dove (p. 20) © Sakepaint
Full Moon Night (p. 23) © Tomasz Zaida
Joaquín Rodrigo (p. 28) © Cecilia Rodrigo
Nail Files (p. 35) © kolesnikovserg
Woman Dancing (p. 36) © konradbak
Traditional Japanese Flute (p. 64) © brizmaker
Black Metal Music Stand (p. 68) © sdubrov
Guitar foot stool (p. 68) © Upsidedowncake
Capodaster (p. 68) © galira
Metronome (p. 68) © Balz Kure
Classical Guitar Strings (p. 68) © designelements
All others: Archive Schott Music GmbH & Co KG

Audio Recording
Recording artist: Carl Herring
Recording producer: Chiaki Yamazaki
Recording engineer: Naito Terukazu, Bazooka Studio, Takadanobaba, Tokyo

Layout: Chloë Alexander Design / Ulrike Speyer

© 2018 Schott Music Ltd., London
Printed in Germany • S&Co9356

CONTENTS

About Miloš Karadaglić 5
About This Book 6
How to Use This Book 7
My Journey 8

Spanish Romance 12
    My Daily Warm-Up 14
Eventide 16
    Five-note Scales 17
The Girl From Far Away 18
Peace 20
    Getting a Great Tone 20
    Chord Corner 1 22
Beautiful Moonlight 23
    Chord Corner 2 25
    The Natural Minor Scale 26
    Using a Capo 26
Aeolian Mode 27
Españoleta (Rodrigo) 38
    Mastering The Fretboard 30
Ode to Joy (An die Freude) 32
    Learning the language of music
    with MELUDIA 34
    Nails 35
Malagueña 36
    The Building Blocks of Music 38
Allegro (Mozart) 40
The Trout (Die Forelle) 42
    Developing Speed 44

Brigands Were Dancing 45
    Slurs 46
**Two 19th-century Guitar Heroes:
Sor & Giuliani** 47
Leçon (Sor) 48
Écossaise in A minor (Giuliani) 49
    The Barré 50
    A Universal Sound 51
Canto 52
    Using Barrés 52
    Improvisation 52
    Chord Corner 3: A Jazz "Turnaround" 53
Mundo Vivo 54
    Percussion 54
Menuett I (Bach) 56
    Chord Corner 4 58
    Slurs and Ornaments 59
    The Baroque Guitar 60
Canario 61
Pastime with Good Company 62
    Harmonics 63
Song of the Seashore 64
Congratulations 66
Discography 67
Recommended Accessories 68
Glossary 68
How to read Tablature (TAB) 71
Fretboard Map 72

ABOUT MILOŠ KARADAGLIĆ

"The hottest guitarist in the world", Miloš Karadaglić continues to top the record charts and delight audiences worldwide. His first three releases on Deutsche Grammophon achieved major chart success around the globe and turned him into "classical music's guitar hero" (BBC Music Magazine) overnight. His 2014 recording of Rodrigo's concertos had the Sunday Times calling him "The King of Aranjuez", while "Blackbird – the Beatles album" (2016) was received with unanimous critical acclaim. Recorded in the infamous Abbey Road Studio 2, it features classic Beatles-songs performed in innovative new arrangements by Sérgio Assad and includes collaborations with the jazz legend Gregory Porter, pop singer Tori Amos, cellist Steven Isserlis and sitar superstar Anoushka Shankar.

Miloš has worked with many of the world's leading orchestras and conductors and performed in the greatest concert venues around the globe. He is the first ever guitarist to have played a solo recital at the Royal Albert Hall in London, The Guardian commenting: "More extraordinary by far, however, was the way a single guitarist, playing an intimate and understated set, and equipped with a single microphone and some clever lighting, could shrink the Hall's cavernous space into something so close." The Independent concluded: "Defying its many critics to offer a dramatic and rounded evening of classical music, the guitar itself was the breakout star here – a sleight of hand that makes Karadaglić not only a magician, but a serious and accomplished musician".

In the current season Miloš will curate a musical journey through the repertoire that has been most important to him so far in his life and career- a programme that sees him perform solo and with various ensembles throughout the United Kingdom, Europe, Asia and the United States.

Now firmly established in the classical firmament, Miloš remains committed to commissioning new repertoire, especially when it comes to the repertoire for guitar and orchestra. Next season will mark the world premiere of Canadian composer Howard Shore's first ever guitar concerto. It was commissioned for him by the National Arts Centre Orchestra Ottawa and Alexander Shelley. Further new commissions for Miloš include a concerto by composer Joby Talbot which will be premiered in August 2018 at the BBC Proms Festival in London.

Miloš is a passionate supporter of music education and acts as a Patron of the Mayor of London Fund for Young Musicians and the Awards for Young Musicians. He is an Ambassador for Live Music Now and the Wigmore Hall's Learning Programme. He is also a brand ambassador for the luxury Swiss watchmaker Raymond Weil. Taking every opportunity to promote classical music to the widest possible audience, Miloš often finds himself in the role of radio and TV presenter, having recently appeared as a mentor for the nationwide talent competition Guitar Star on Sky Arts, in addition to co-presenting the 2014 BBC Young Musician of the Year.

Born in Montenegro in 1983, Miloš first started playing the guitar at the age of 8. At 16, he successfully applied for a scholarship to study at the Royal Academy of Music where he studied with professor Michael Lewin and moved to London where he continues to live while keeping close ties with his family and homeland. He was appointed a Fellow of the Royal Academy of Music in 2015. He performs on a 2007 Greg Smallman guitar.

ABOUT THIS BOOK

Welcome to Play Guitar With Miloš, Level 1!

I'M SO EXCITED about this book! It's packed with great pieces from a wide range of styles and periods. Many are completely unique to this book, but you'll find some familiar favourites too – all of which I loved to play as a budding guitarist. For each piece, I'll give you some background information and tell you why they are special to me. I'll also suggest some exercises to help you develop a strong technique, and pass on some of the hints and tips that I found useful over the years.

This book is for anyone wishing to study the guitar, either by themselves or with a teacher. Some of the pieces in this book are duets. If you don't have anyone else to play with, don't worry, there are backing tracks for you to enjoy playing along with.

In terms of **difficulty**, most of the pieces correspond to UK Grades 1 and 2. This is a rough guide only. For example, you will find pieces here that include higher notes than you would traditionally find in Grades 1 and 2 repertoire. High notes may be difficult to read, but they aren't especially difficult to play. For our purposes here though, there is no good reason to exclude them – all for more variety and fun.

Being familiar with the common chord shapes is extremely useful for all guitarists. I'll help you build a good stock of chords and we'll link them to the pieces you're playing. Noticing chord shapes in the pieces you play will deepen your understanding of the music and will help you learn the pieces more quickly and easily. Having a broad selection of chord shapes at your fingertips also opens doors for you to enjoy other styles of guitar playing.

This book assumes that you already have at least a basic understanding of music theory, such as knowing the names of notes in the treble clef, and being able to read simple rhythms and common key signatures. You'll find a fretboard map on page 72 to help you locate pitches on the guitar itself.

Take your time, practise regularly, enjoy the journey! Let's get started and good luck!

HOW TO USE THIS BOOK

When you see this symbol, visit **www.playguitarwithmilos.com** to hear a recording. For the duet pieces, you'll hear two versions: a full version, and a version with just the accompaniment for you to play along with.

Accompaniment parts and full scores for the duets are available for download from **www.playguitarwithmilos.com**.

Aeolian mode   Some words are in bold the first time they appear. This means you'll find them in the glossary on page 69. Check the glossary too for any symbols of notation you're not familiar with.

TAB (tablature)

In this book, tablature (TAB) is used sparingly, mostly only in the introduction to some pieces as a quick and convenient way to locate notes. I believe that tablature is limited in its musical scope and that it's far better to become confident at reading standard notation than to rely on tablature. So, we generally won't use it for full pieces, and will gradually discontinue its use altogether as we progress. See page 71 for a summary of how to read tablature.

[♩ = 90]   Metronome marks in brackets indicate my own suggested tempo, and are intended only as a rough guide. Those without brackets are the composer's or arranger's original indications.

Technical slurs (pull-offs and hammer-ons) are shown by a dashed line.

MY JOURNEY

I WAS BORN and grew up in a small Balkan Republic called Montenegro. When I was a child, Montenegro was part of Yugoslavia. I grew up in a small but very devoted family, and had parents that supported my brother and me in every way they possibly could. I was always a very curious child and my parents encouraged me to explore my interests. At the age of eight, out of the blue, I asked my father to take me to the music school. It was really because I had seen a guy on TV playing guitar and I thought he was the coolest person ever. Also, I was not very good on the football pitch and I couldn't score a goal to save my life. Hence the idea of playing guitar brilliantly answered to my poor skills as a footballer.

So I ended up in the music school, and my instrument was the old guitar from our home that had been forgotten by everyone. The moment I found it, I found my best friend. At the music school, the teachers were pretty serious: grow long nails, learn to read music, take solfeggio lessons. Very quickly I became bored. When I was just about to give up and all the teachers said they couldn't tame me, my father had an idea. In his collection of LPs, somewhere among the Rolling Stones and Bee Gees records, he discovered a recording of a guitar recital by the great Andrés Segovia. He played me a piece from the album, and when I heard it, I was instantly transported. I thought that this was the most amazing, magical sound. It became my mission to learn to play guitar like that. The piece was *Asturias* by Isaac Albéniz. Many years later, when I released my first album for Deutsche Grammophon, I made sure that *Asturias* was the first track. This is how my love affair with the classical guitar really began.

Once I was committed to the classical guitar and had played my first public concert, I discovered that I absolutely loved being on stage. To this day, this is what inspires me the most. It is what inspires me to continue afresh every day, to look always for the higher meaning, all in order to be the best artist and the best musician that I can possibly be. Music is the universal language of the world. I feel so blessed and privileged to have been given a purpose in life from such a young age.

At seventeen, I came to study at the Royal Academy of Music in London. In those days, going from Montenegro to London felt to me a bit like going to the Moon. This was a very challenging time in my life, but fast forward a few years, and there I was, ready to face the world as a serious artist. I recorded a CD, sent it everywhere, and played lots of small local concerts. I knocked on many doors, and everyone kept saying that as a classical guitarist, one can't really have a major career. I found that extremely odd, because I knew people who did, and even more than that, I knew that the guitar was the most popular instrument in the whole world! I don't know a single person who hasn't at some point in their life tried a guitar. So I kept believing in myself and believing that I could do it.

And I did. After a lot of hard work and a little bit of luck, I signed to become an exclusive recording artist with the wonderful record label, Deutsche Grammophon. My life changed completely. Within sixteen months, even the Royal Albert Hall was sold out and centre stage was all mine. And yet it had only just begun. What followed was the stuff of dreams; dreams I wish to share with everyone holding this book. And it all begins with knowing how to play this incredible instrument, the classical guitar.

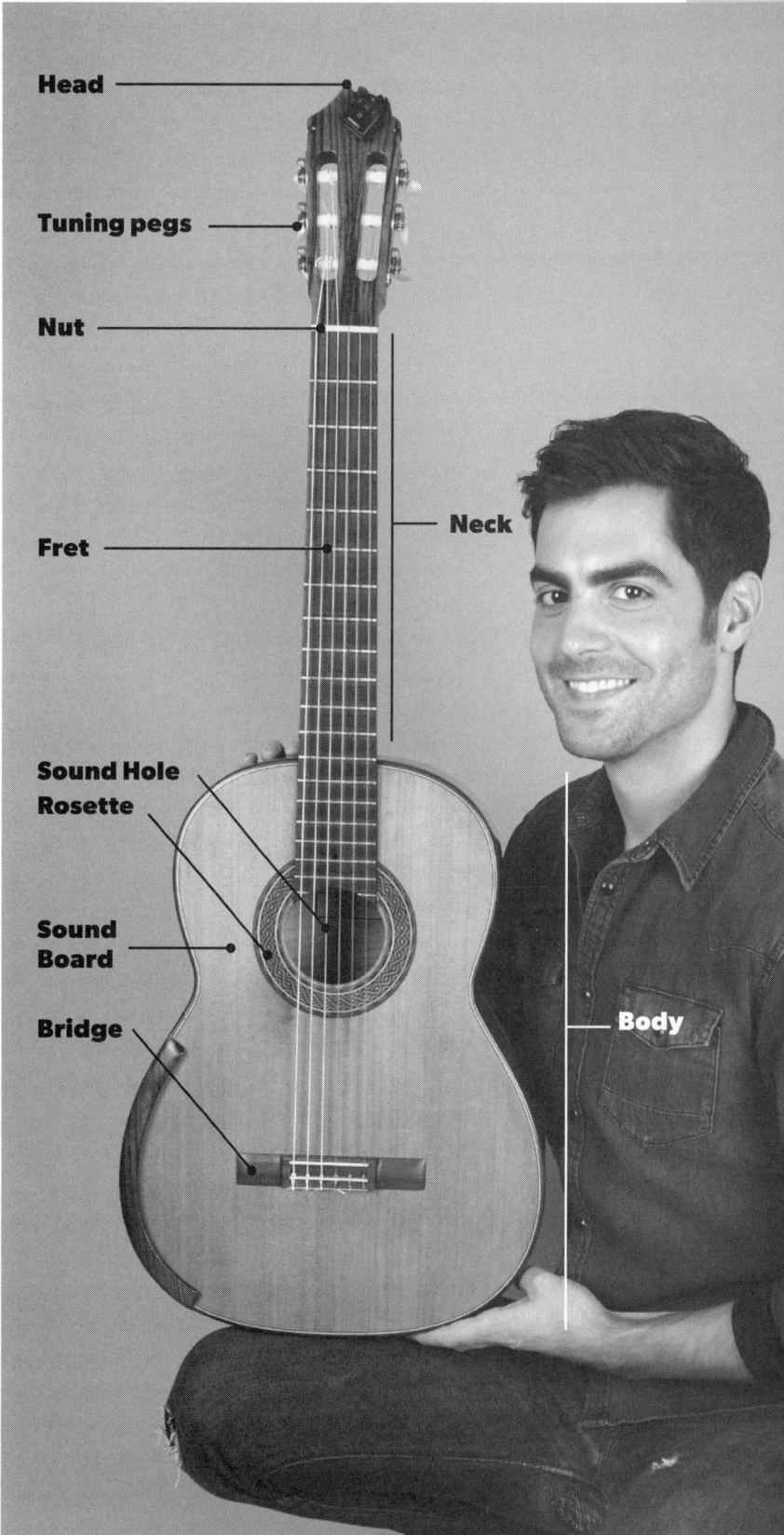

This picture shows you the ideal playing posture.

FINGERING

The fingers of the **left hand** are referred to by numbers. In guitar music, these numbers appear near note heads. Since the left thumb is not usually used for fretting notes, we start counting from the index finger. A zero ("0") means an open string.

The fingers of the **right hand** are referred to by letters. Except for some special, advanced techniques, the right little finger is not used. The letters come from the Spanish names for these fingers:

p = pulgar (thumb)
i = índice (index)
m = medio (middle)
a = anular (ring)

SPANISH ROMANCE

**This is an arrangement of the very first piece I played in public.
I was nine years old and after I'd finished playing, the audience went crazy.
It was probably thanks to this experience that I completely fell in love with being
on stage and was inspired to work hard in order to become a serious concert artist.**

In this book, I want to help you develop a strong technique.
For this first piece however, let's just enjoy playing, without worrying about
technique at all. I deliberately haven't added any fingering[1].

Try playing the whole melody on string ①. I'm sure you know this melody
well, so simply allow your ears to guide your left hand.

You could also play along with my recording of this piece.
It appears on the album *Mediterráneo* (DG 4779338).

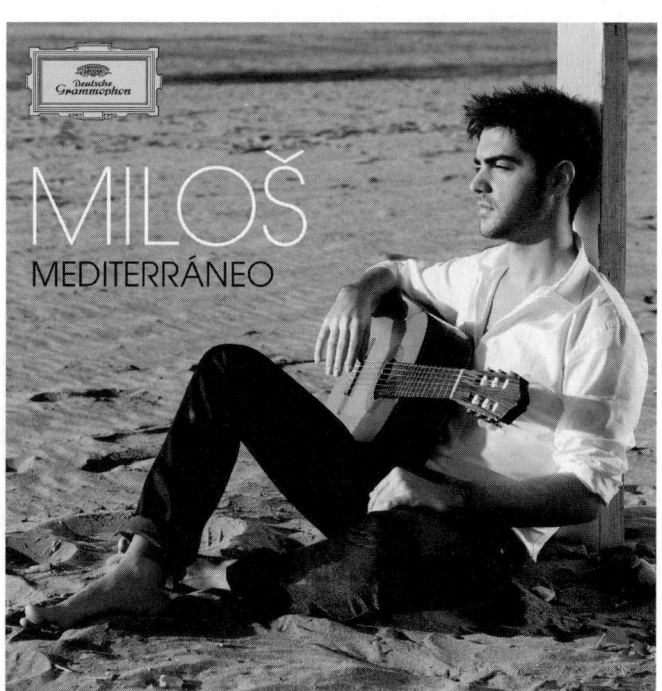

[1] A version with recommended fingering is available as a free download from www.playguitarwithmilos.com

Spanish Romance

 *

01 Audio + PDF of Duet Score

trad. Spanish
arr. Miloš Karadaglić

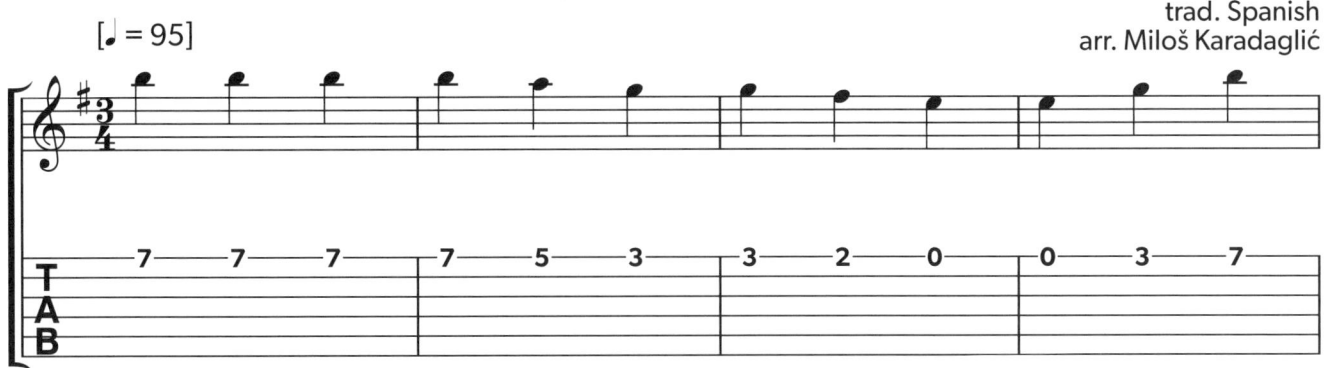

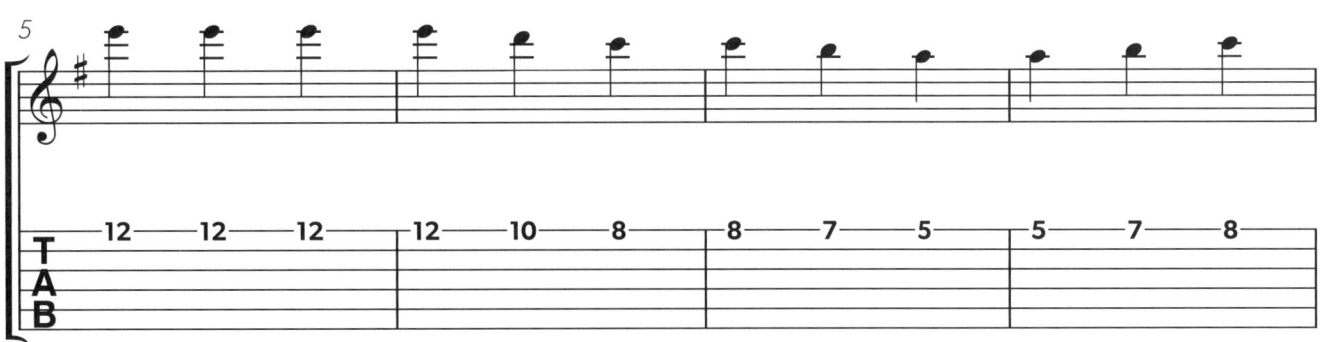

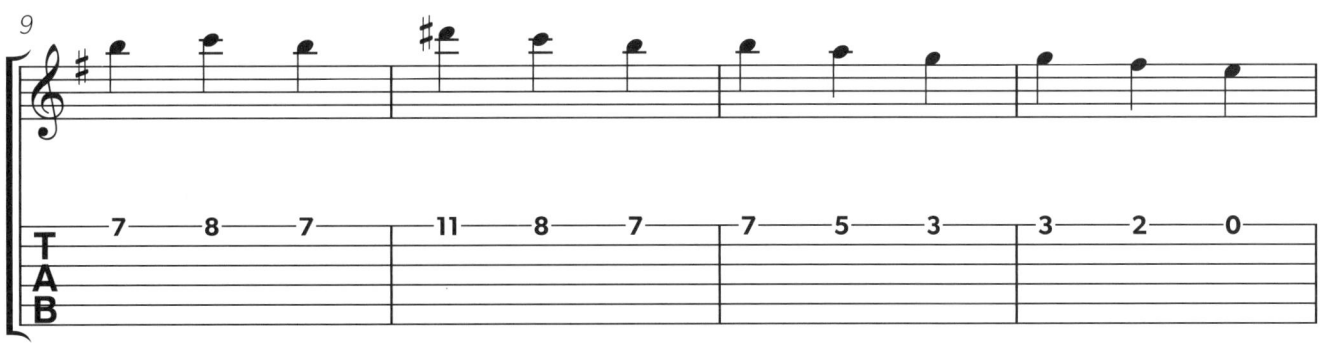

© 2018 Schott Music Ltd., London

* When you see this symbol, visit www.playguitarwithmilos.com to hear a recording and to find accompaniment parts for the pieces arranged as duets.

MY DAILY WARM-UP

Each day, the first time that I pick up my guitar, I take a few moments to warm up gently.
It feels almost like saying a very relaxed 'hello' to a close friend.
I like to take my time, and just enjoy the sensation of my fingers on the strings.

Here's what I do:

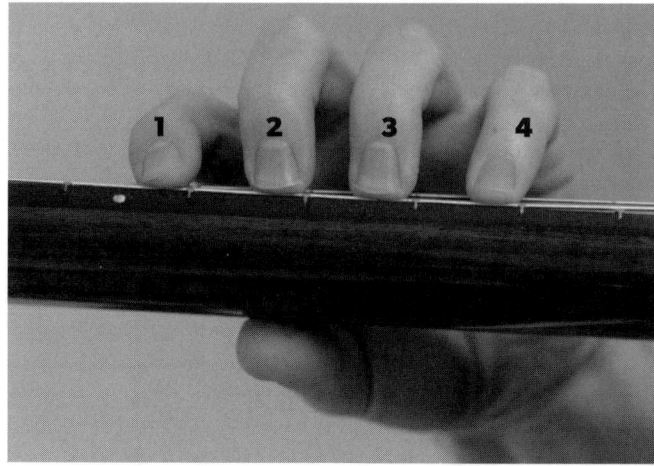

Exercise 1 – Left Hand

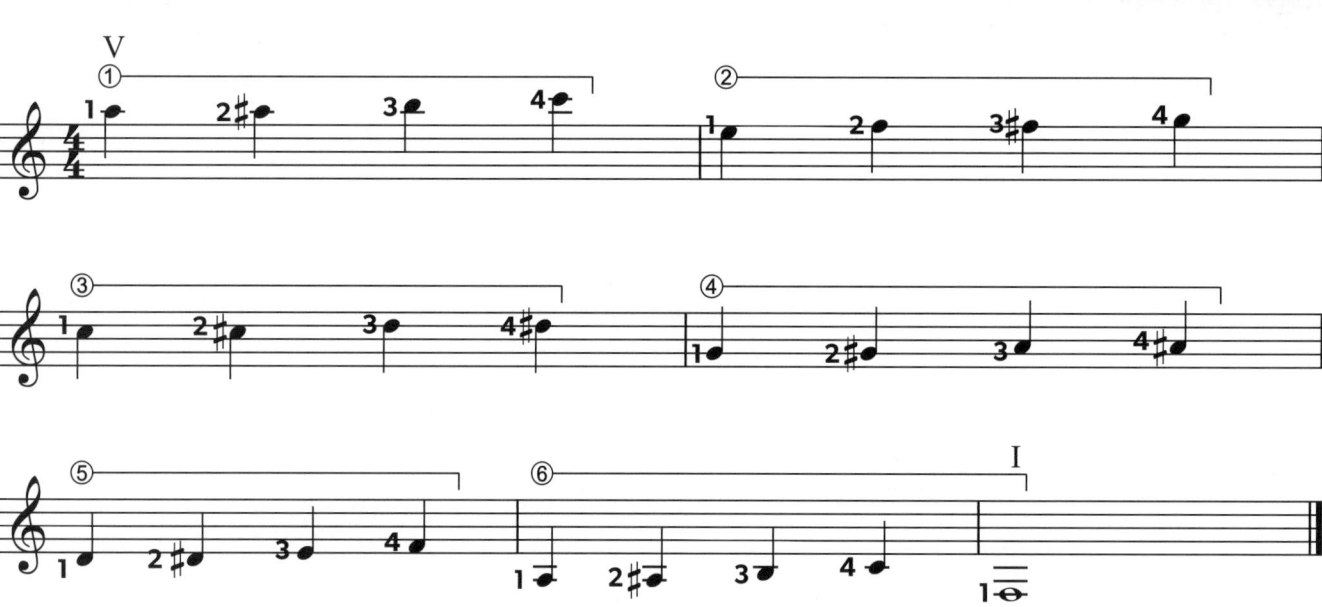

Please see the glossary on p. 69 if you're not sure about any of the symbols used above.

- Keep each finger down for as long as possible.
- Even if a finger isn't currently pressing down, keep it as close to the string as possible.
- Try this exercise backwards too. First plant the fingers, then peel them off one at a time.
- Try the same exercise in different places on the fretboard.

Exercise 2 – Right Hand

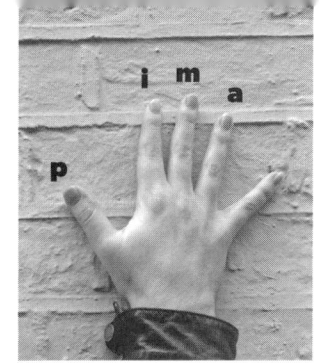

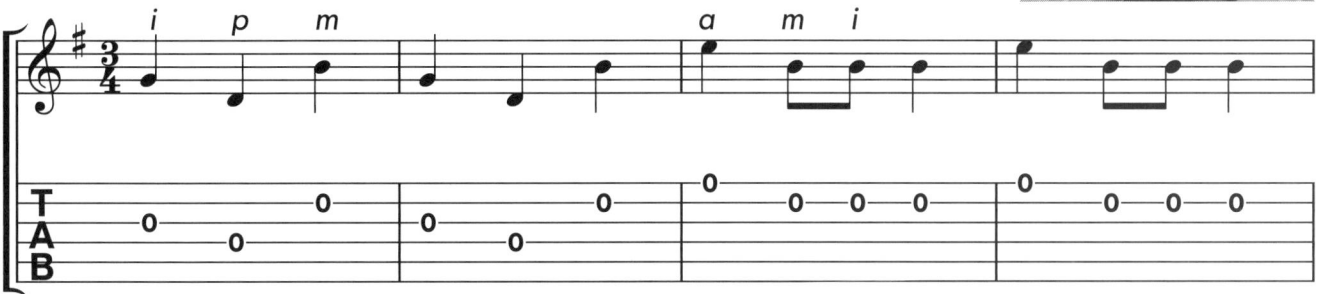

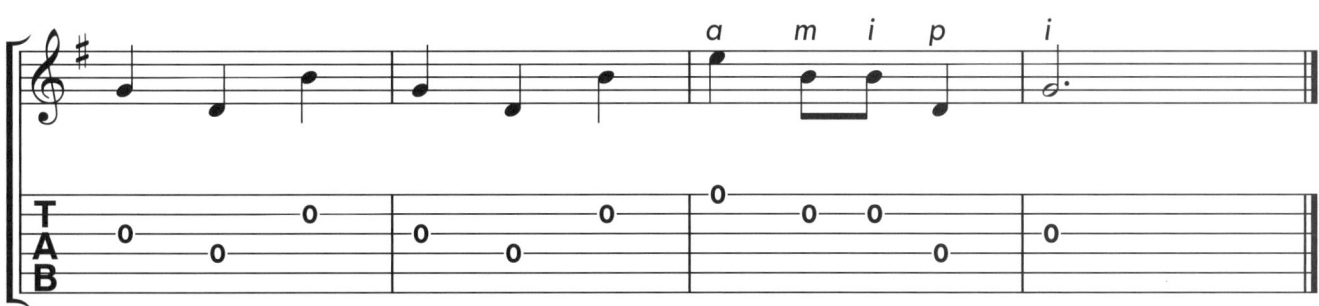

EVENTIDE

Eventide is an example of a truly timeless melody. Best known as the melody of the hymn *Abide With Me*, it has inspired generations of people around the world. It has been used in countless films and TV shows and is played at major sporting events such as the UK Football Association Cup Final.

Eventide follows on nicely from the warm-up you've just done.

Stay in **fifth position** throughout and keep your fingers close to the strings.

Notes used

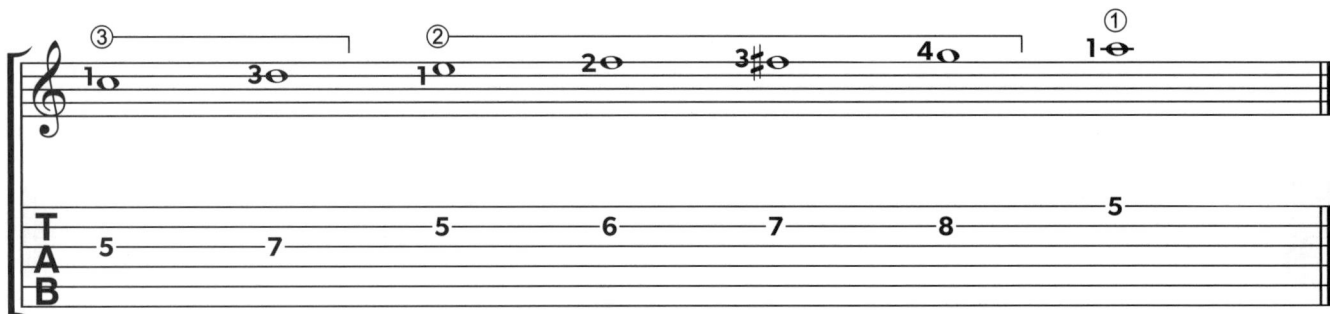

Eventide

02 Audio + PDF of Duet Score

William Henry Monk
(1823-1889)
arr. Carl Herring

© 2018 Schott Music Ltd., London

FIVE-NOTE SCALES

Eventide contains all of the notes used in this five-note scale of C major:

Pattern 1

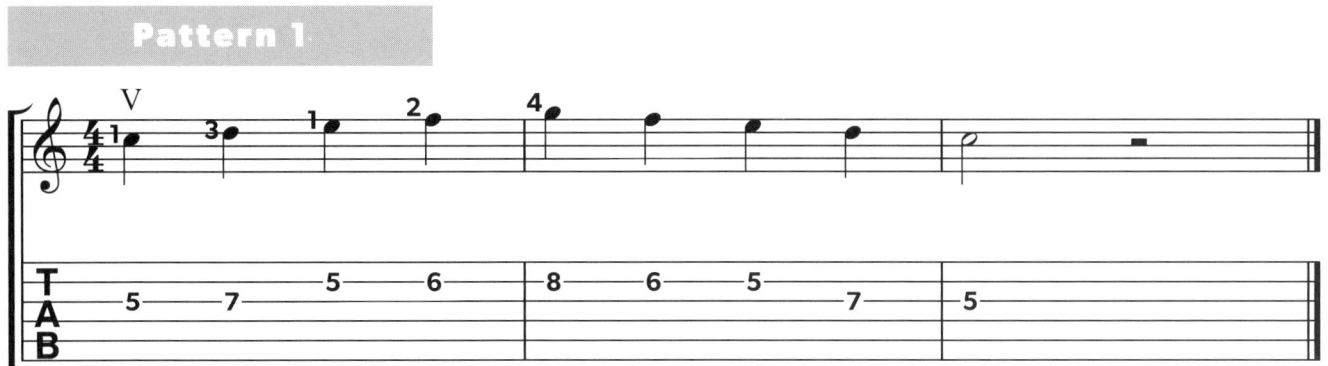

If we play exactly the same pattern of fingering two frets higher, we get a five-note scale of D major:

Pattern 1 in D

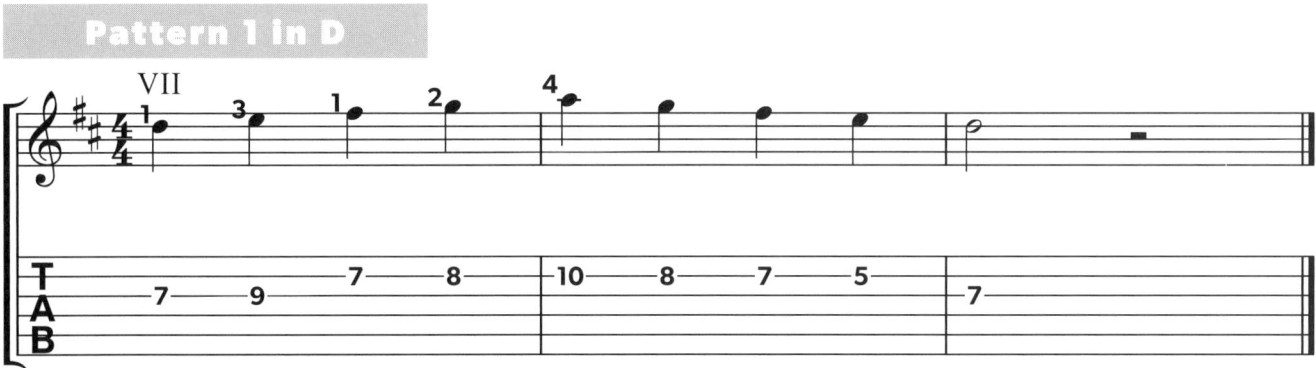

As long as you start on string ③, this pattern will work anywhere on the neck.

But what about if we want to play the scale starting on a different string? In that case, we need a different pattern. The following pattern lets you play a five-note scale on any of the other strings!
Here's D major again, but this time starting on string ②:

Pattern 2

Let's use the same pattern to play a five-note G major scale:

Pattern 2 in G

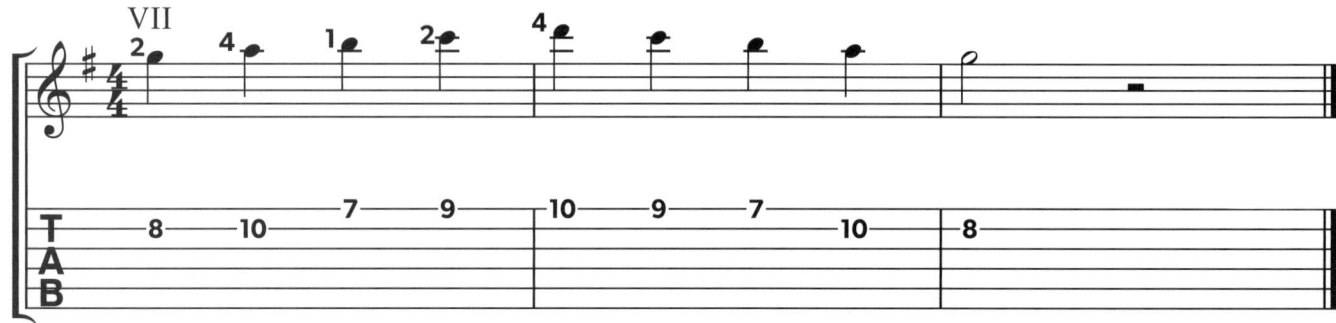

Using just these two patterns, you can now play five-note major scales anywhere on the neck!
Just remember to use the first pattern if you start on string ③.

THE GIRL FROM FAR AWAY

Виђи, виђи мајко *(Viđi, Viđi Majko)*

Montenegrin weddings are always great fun! There is always a lot of wonderful food and of course, endless singing and dancing! The lyrics of this wedding song are about a man introducing his bride to his mother for the first time. It's sort of a Montenegrin "Meet the Parents!"

You can play the whole of *The Girl from Far Away* using just the five-note scale of G major you played above.

Just to be sure – here it is again:

Notes used

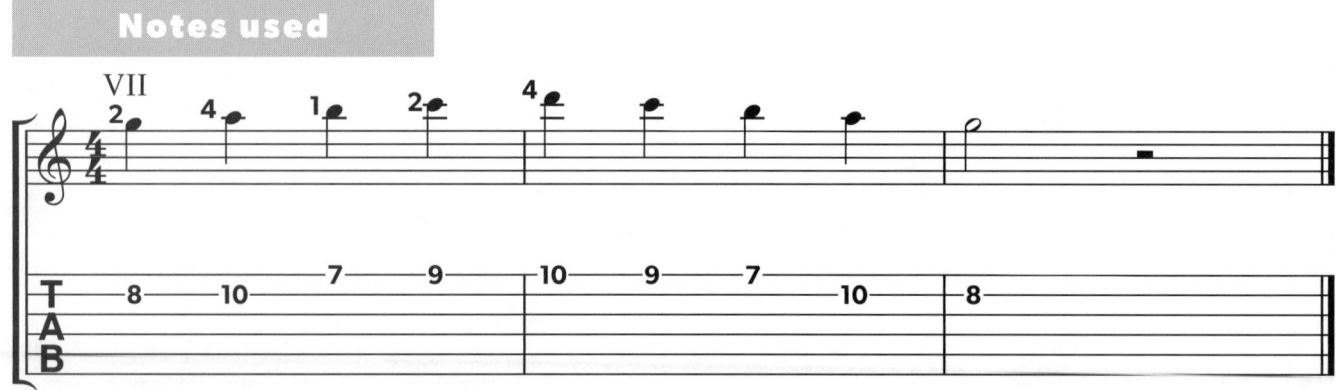

Bars 13 - 17: If you find these rhythms difficult, please listen to the recording to get used to how this part of the piece goes.

The Girl from Far Away
Виђи, виђи мајко (Viđi, Viđi Majko)

03 Audio + PDF of Duet Score

trad. Montenegrin
arr. Carl Herring

D. S. al Fine

Fine

© 2018 Schott Music Ltd., London

PEACE*

There are so many conflicts in the world today, and as someone who grew up in times of unrest, I feel that this piece is a beautiful reminder that music is the language of the world even when all else fails.

In the early stages of my career, I very much enjoyed teaching young children. **Rounds** like this one were always popular with students because of the wonderful sound that is created by two or more people playing together.

Once you know this piece well, try playing it with friends:

- Player two starts when player one has reached the first star (bar 9).
- Player three starts when player one has reached the second star (bar 17).
- When you reach the end, go back to the beginning.

Keep a steady **pulse** and enjoy the way your sound blends with that of your friends.

Getting a Great Tone

Plant **p**, **i**, **m** and **a**, give the strings a squeeze. Notice how your wrist comes out a little.

- Push each string towards the soundboard a little as you play it. This will give you a full, round sound.

* This piece is most commonly known by its Latin title, *Dona Nobis Pacem*. When sung, the lyrics consist simply of these three words, translating as *Give Us Peace*.

Peace
Dona Nobis Pacem

anon.
arr. Carl Herring

© 2018 Schott Music Ltd., London

CHORD CORNER 1

Certain chord progressions appear again and again in music. In pop music, one of the most enduring ones is: I-V-vi-IV. In the key of G, this gives us: G-D(7)-Em (E minor)-C. Does it sound familiar?*

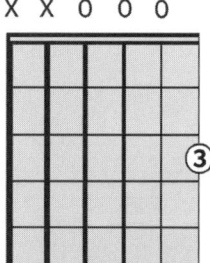
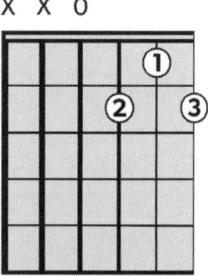
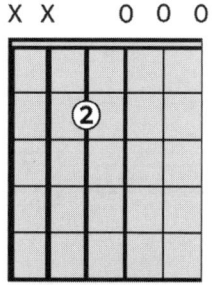
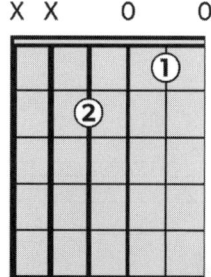

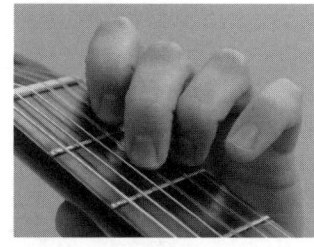
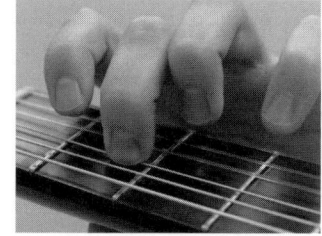

*By the way, I've changed D to D7 because it's slightly easier to play and sounds effective here.

You can hear this progression in the song *Let It Be*, from my Beatles album *Blackbird*. Here are some famous songs that use related progressions:

I-V-vi-IV

- *With Or Without You* – U2
- *Someone Like You* (chorus) – Adele

I-vi-IV-V

- *Stand By Me* – Ben E. King
- *Blue Moon* – Richard Rogers

vi-IV-I-V

- *If I Were A Boy* – Beyonce
- *It's My Life* – Bon Jovi
- *Poker Face* – Lady Gaga

For further examples, try typing **I-V-vi-IV** into an internet search engine.

BEAUTIFUL MOONLIGHT

Ніч яка місячна *(Nich Yaka Misyachna)*

Many pieces of classical music were inspired by beautiful scenery. As the title suggests, this piece is a fine example of that. It very much reminds me of the famous *Spanish Romance* **which appears at the beginning of this book and which you'll learn in full in book three of this series. It might even be that this charming Ukrainian folk song was the inspiration for it!**

To prepare for playing thumb and fingers together:

- Learn and play the melody and bass parts separately.
- Sing the melody while you play the bass part.

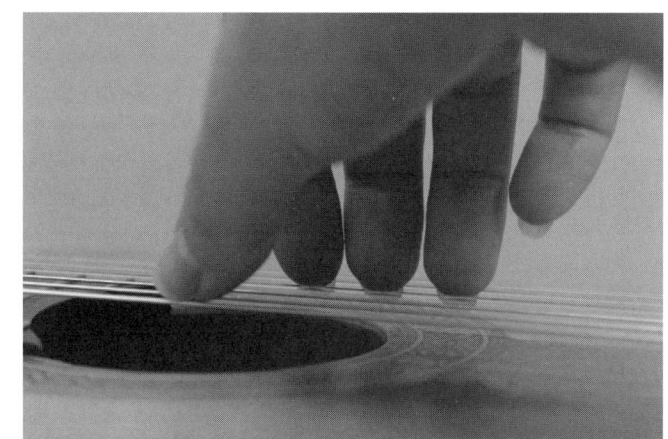

- Try the following exercises:

Open string exercises

© 2018 Schott Music Ltd., London

As you did with *Peace*, **keep your wrist out a little and aim for a full, round tone**

Beautiful Moonlight
Ніч яка місячна (Nich Yaka Misyachna)

05 Audio

Mykola Lysenko
1842-1912
arr. Carl Herring

© 2018 Schott Music Ltd., London

CHORD CORNER 2

The chords of A minor and E are what are called *lookalike* shapes. By moving the same basic shape to a different place on the guitar, you can sometimes discover some very interesting sounds. Try this with any new chord shape that you learn. Experiment and have fun!

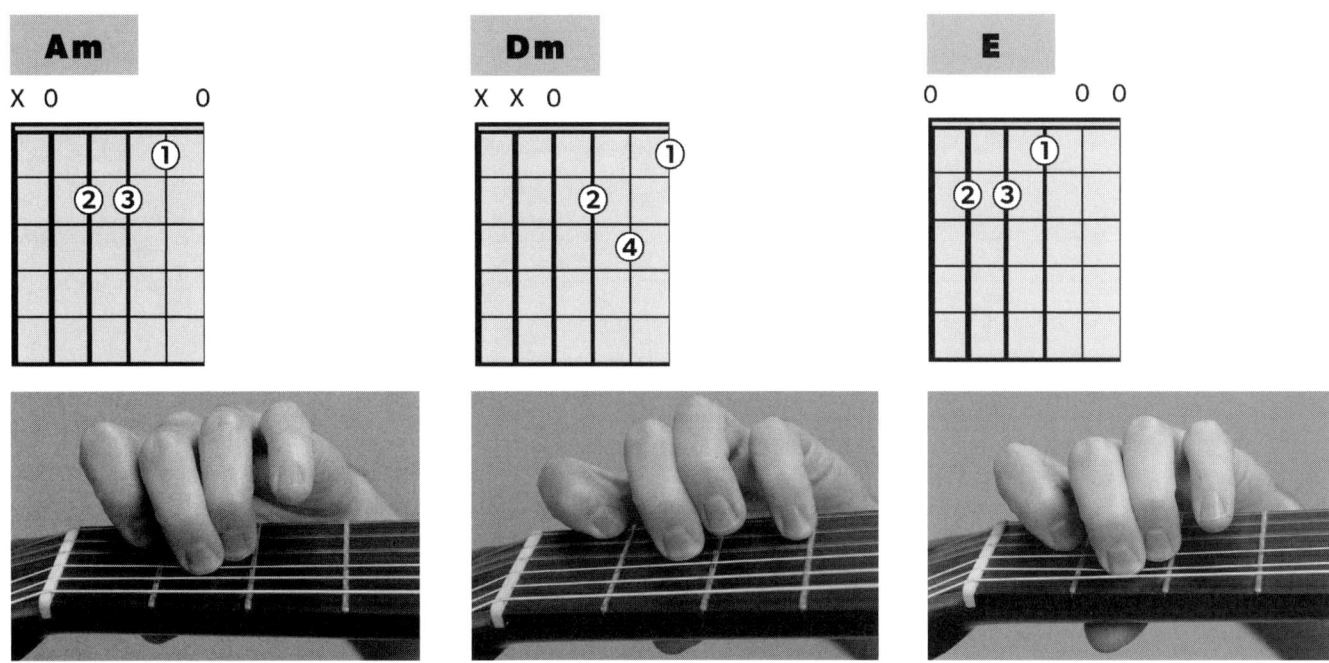

The three chords above form a set. In the key of A minor, we can label them as chords i, iv and V. This set is very common, and you'll hear it a lot in the folk music of Eastern Europe.

Beautiful Moonlight (accompaniment)

Strum this chord accompaniment to *Beautiful Moonlight* (p. 24) while you hum the melody.
Strum once for each three-beat bar.

Am	Am	E	E
E	E	Am	Am
Am	Am	Dm	Dm
E	E	Am	Am

THE NATURAL MINOR SCALE

If we start on A and continue stepwise without adding any sharps or flats, we get a natural minor scale. This is also known as the *Aeolian mode*. I find it has quite a pure, ancient sound. Notice how in the following piece, the composer uses only notes from this scale.

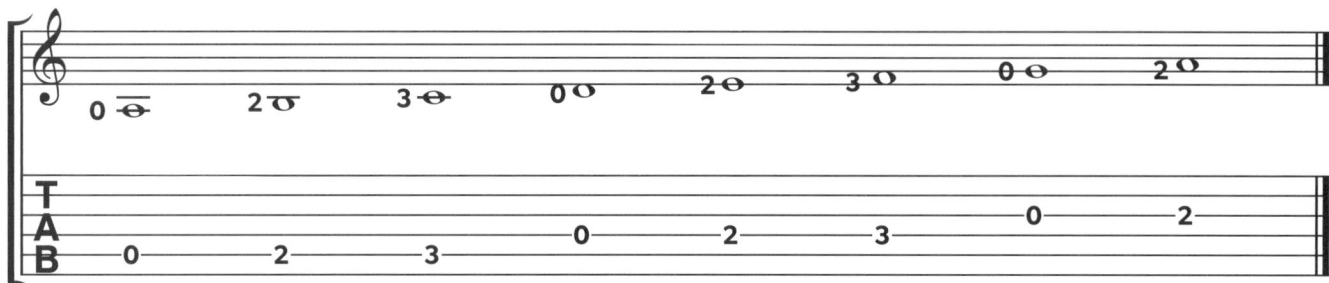

Aeolian Mode

An arch after some of the bass notes, indicates that those notes should ring on over the others. In the last two lines of the piece, try to sustain the bass notes by keeping your third finger pressed down for as long as possible. If this stretch is difficult, you'll find that using a **capo** on the second, third, or fourth fret makes it much easier.

Also, if you don't already use a footstool, you'll probably find that using one makes stretches like these easier. Check out the picture on page 10 for guidance on how to sit properly.

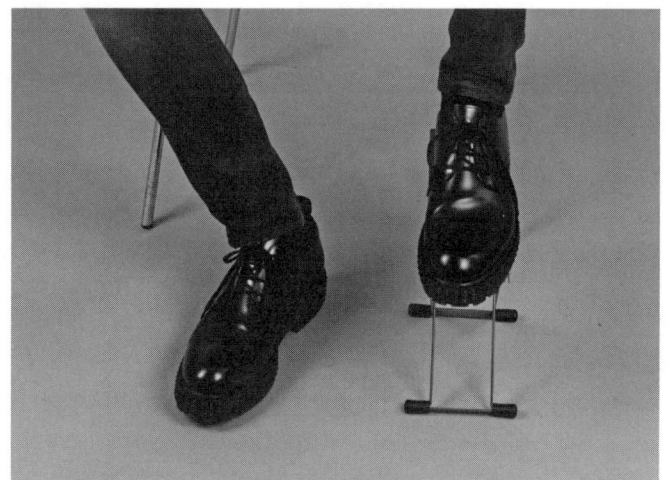

Using a Capo

As mentioned above, using a capo can make certain pieces easier to play. The reason for this is that higher up the neck, the frets become closer together and it becomes easier to depress the strings. Feel free to experiment with a capo whenever you come across difficult stretches in a low position.

Another reason guitarists use capos is so that they can raise the pitch of a piece without needing to change any fingerings. Think of it like moving the nut.

This is useful if, for example, you want to adjust to the pitch of a singer's voice without having to change the chords you play.

See Appendix on page 6 for my recommendations for various accessories, including capos and footstools.

Aeolian Mode
An ancient Greek scale

06 Audio

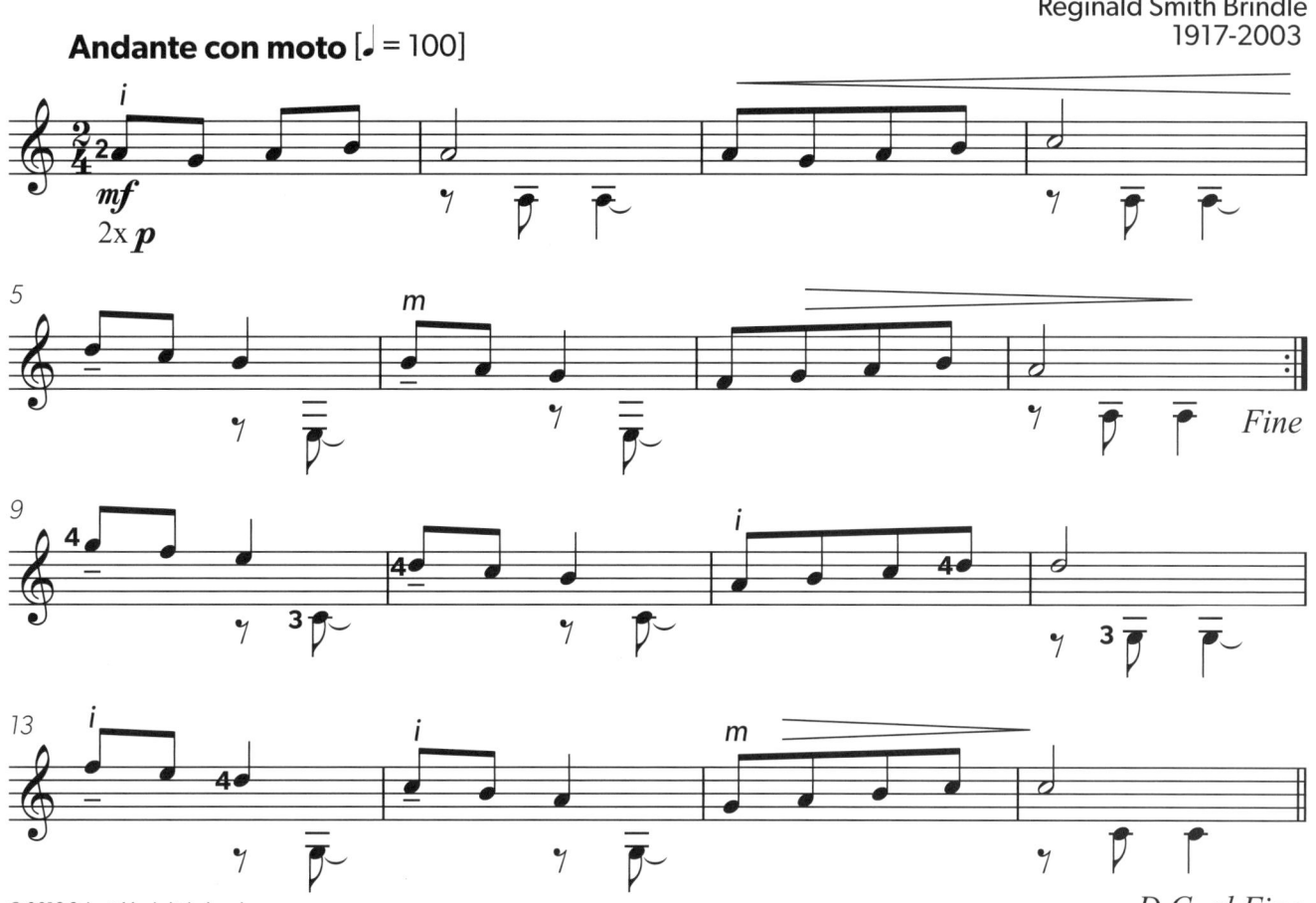

Reginald Smith Brindle
1917-2003

© 2018 Schott Music Ltd., London

ESPAÑOLETA

from *Fantasia Para Un Gentilhombre*, movement II

Joaquín Rodrigo gave the guitar one of its greatest and most treasured pieces, the sublime *Concierto de Aranjuez* for guitar and orchestra. It's a real rite of passage for any classical guitarist, and we'll take a look at some excerpts from it in books 3 and 4 of this series.

Andrés Segovia was the most famous classical guitarist of his time. Unfortunately for him, the *Concierto de Aranjuez* ended up being dedicated to another guitarist. This prompted Rodrigo to write another concerto, which he called *Fantasia Para Un Gentilhombre* (Fantasia for a Gentleman). The gentleman in question was of course Segovia. Those two concertos are the crown jewels of guitar repertoire.

The second movement of *Fantasia Para Un Gentilhombre* contains several contrasting themes, but it opens with an *Españoleta* (an old Spanish dance).

This haunting melody is in the bass and should be played entirely by the thumb.

Joaquín Rodrigo

Españoleta
from *Fantasia Para Un Gentilhombre*, movement II

07 Audio

Joaquín Rodrigo
1901-1999

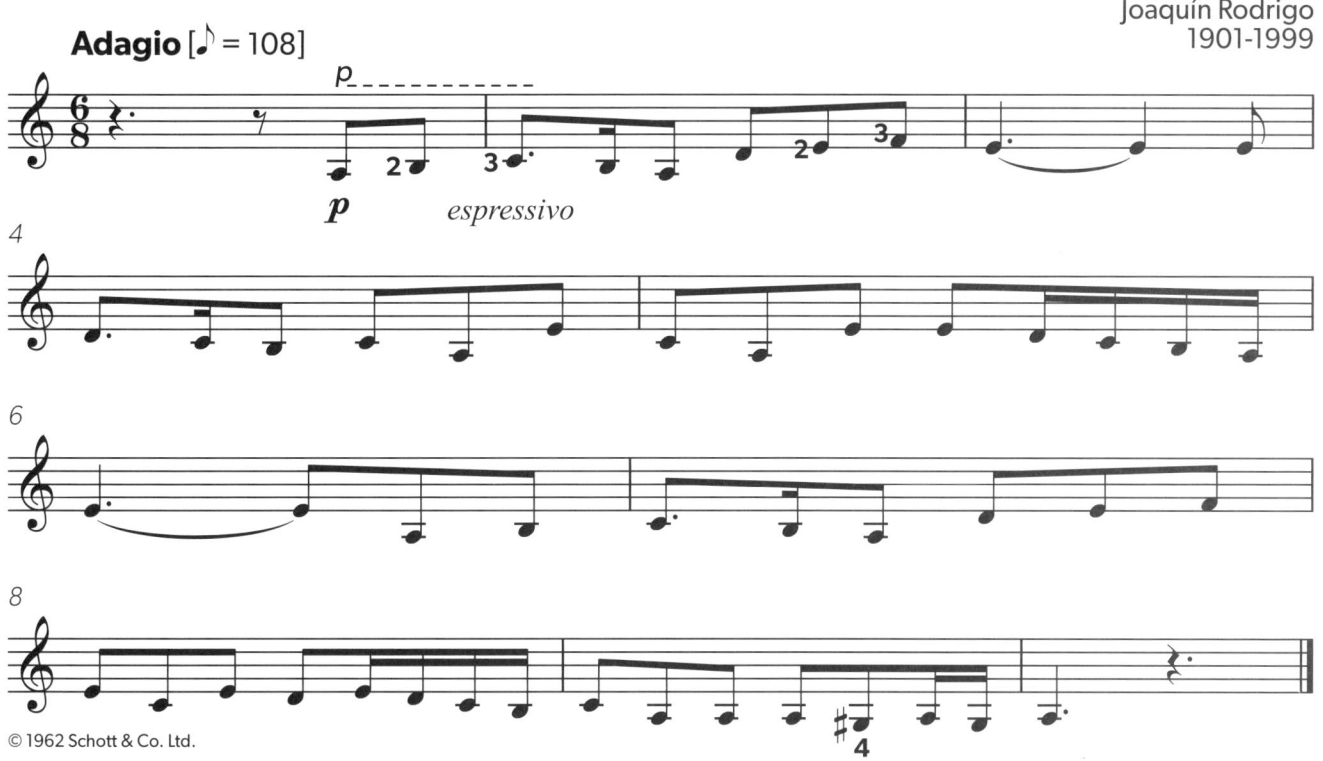

© 1962 Schott & Co. Ltd.

You can hear both of these concertos on my album
Miloš: Aranjuez (DG 4810811).

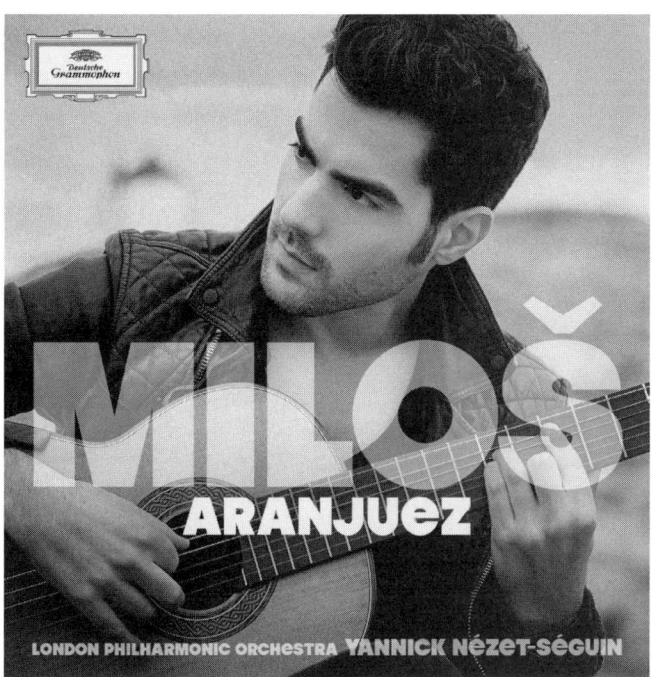

MASTERING THE FRETBOARD

Understandably, many guitarists feel daunted by the prospect of having to memorise the entire fretboard. The best way to approach this is to look for recurring fingering patterns in the music that you play. To illustrate what I mean, let's look again at the five-note scale shapes we learned on page 17. We can use the second of those patterns to play the following E major scale:

Exercise 1

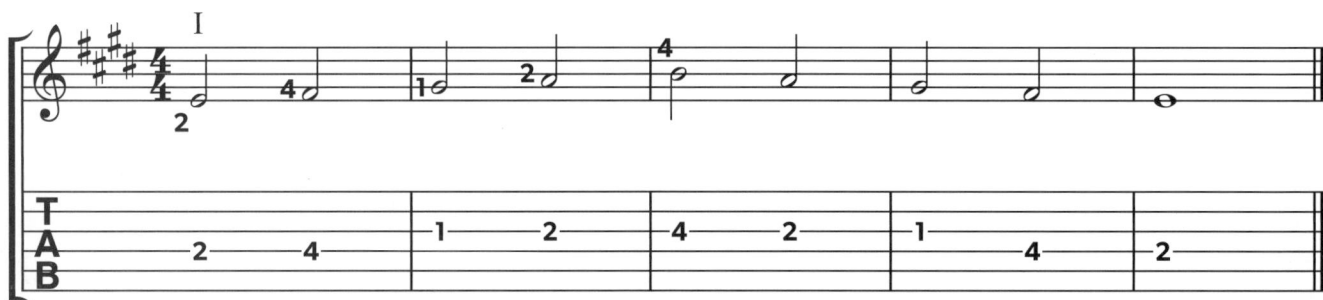

Now play the same notes in sixth position, using exactly the same fingering.
Notice the subtle change in tone quality or **timbre**.

Exercise 2

If we play the same notes in fourth position, we must change the fingering pattern:

Exercise 3

Which way do you prefer? Try out each of these fingerings with the exercise below.

Exercise 4

ODE TO JOY

An die Freude from *Symphony No. 9*

It's hard now to imagine life without recorded sound. It's everywhere! However, in the past, the best way to enjoy popular melodies at home was either to play them yourself or listen to someone else play them. The guitar was predominantly an instrument enjoyed at home. It's no surprise then that throughout history, it's been very popular to arrange famous themes for the classical guitar. There are many examples of this, some of which will appear in later books of this series.

Here is a truly iconic theme from Beethoven's last symphony, in which he calls for the unity of mankind.

In this arrangement, this inspiring melody appears in the bass.

PRO TIP

Play the thumb part alone before adding the upper part.
As you did with the scales on page 17, try playing this whole piece in positions I, IV and VI.
I personally like the sound and feel of position VI. How about you?
If you find the stretches difficult in position I, use a capo.

Ode to Joy
An die Freude from *Symphony No. 9*

08 Audio

Ludwig van Beethoven
1770-1827
arr. Martin Hegel

© 2018 Schott Music Ltd., London

LEARNING THE LANGUAGE OF MUSIC WITH MELUDIA

Dear student,

Like every musician, I passionately love my instrument. It is part of me and the means through which I express the language of music.

I realised very early on in my musical studies that technically mastering the instrument was, on its own, not enough to become a complete and accomplished musician.

Music is a language and while we can often master the technical challenges of the instrument, we too often overlook or minimize the equal importance of mastering the fundamentals of the language of music.

Many of us have studied **ear training** and/or solfege in school and for many of us, including me, this was an arduous and unenjoyable experience. It shouldn't be and it doesn't have to be this way!

Hence I want to bring to your attention a web and mobile platform that I found extremely useful myself. It is called **MELUDIA** and it allows you to develop your listening skills in a fun and totally private way. By just using it for fifteen or twenty minutes per day, four or five days per week, you will quickly see that your abilities at listening and understanding chords, intervals and rhythms develop further and your confidence as a musician increases.

Meludia is available as a website and as a mobile app, with hundreds of progressive fun exercises aiming to develop your ability to train your musical brain to the highest level. They all complement each other and bring you closer and closer to what we consider a well-trained ear.

To discover more about both the web application and the mobile application, go to:

www.meludia.com

I wish you as much fun and success with Meludia as I have had with it myself.

NAILS

On the fretting hand, nails should always be neatly trimmed. But should we play with nails on the plucking hand? This question has been discussed by guitarists for centuries. Some players, notably Fernando Sor (1778-1839), played entirely without nails. However, the consensus among today's professional guitarists is to use them. They facilitate greater volume, speed and clarity required for concerts.

The question of the ideal length and shape is hotly debated, but everyone agrees on the following points:

- The shape should allow you to strike the string with a combination of nail and flesh.

- The nail edge should be as smooth as possible. Having shaped the nail with an emery board, use a nail buffer to achieve a glassy-smooth finish.

To some extent, the ideal shape and length for you will depend on your nail type.

If you want to try using nails, experiment to find a length and shape that works for you. If you feel that it's not important for you to use nails at the moment, that's fine too!

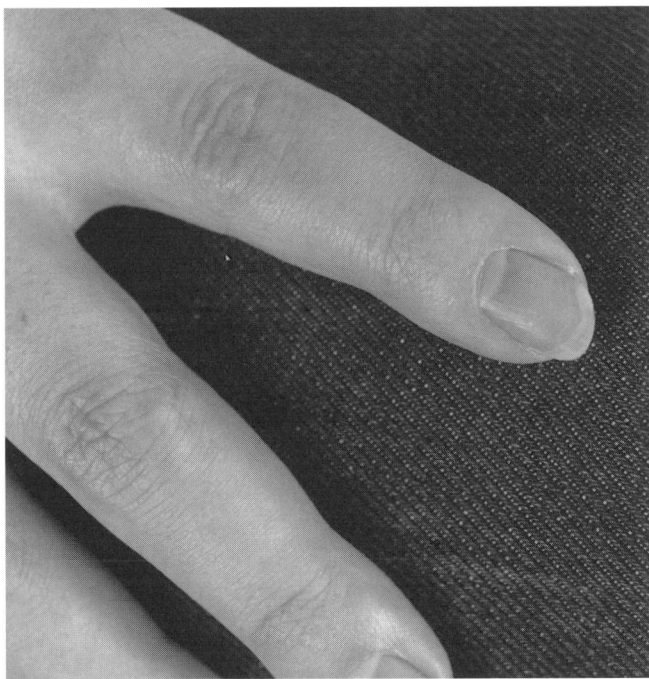
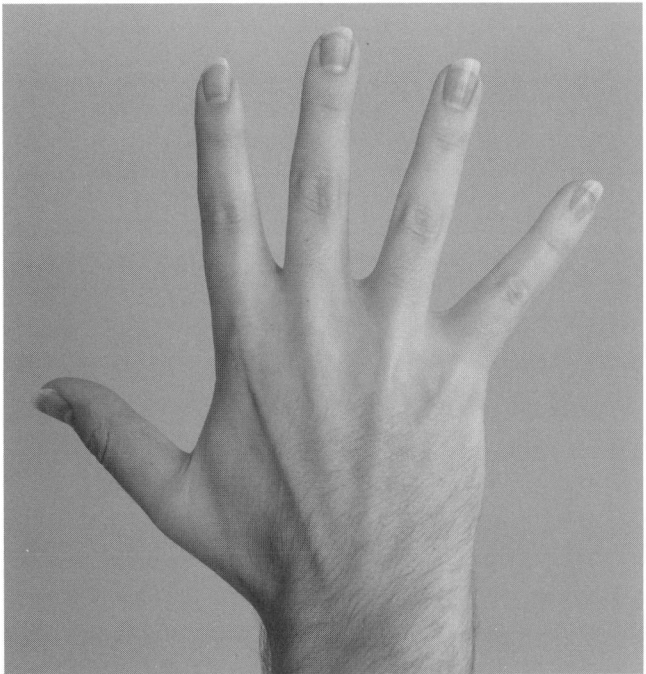

MALAGUEÑA

Malagueña **was the first piece that really excited me. I was eight years old. I remember coming home after a class, practising it and feeling as if my fingers were flying. After that, whoever came to visit us had no choice but to listen to it.**

Flamenco, from which this piece is derived, is the folk music of southern Spain. Pieces like this instantly transport us to a Spanish *fiesta*.

A flamenco guitarist playing this piece would use **rest strokes** for the notes played with the thumb. This produces a very powerful sound. Be sure to try this, but if you find it awkward, using **free stroke** in the thumb is fine too. For the scales in the last two lines, rest stroke (with the fingers) is very effective too.

In bar 4, we have a **natural** sign: (♮). This means that the G in this bar is a 'normal G', or 'G natural'. In this case it is there as a reminder not to play a G♯. We might easily have done so because of the G♯s in the first two bars. The natural sign can also be used to cancel sharps or flats within a bar.

Malagueña

09 Audio

trad. from Spain
arr. Peter Ansorge,
Bruno Szordikowski

© 2018 Schott Music Ltd., London

D.C. al Fine

THE BUILDING BLOCKS OF MUSIC

Let's look again at the five-note scale we learned on page 17. We can use the first pattern to play a five-note scale of A major. As always, say the name of each note as you play it:

We could also choose to use the open strings available to us:

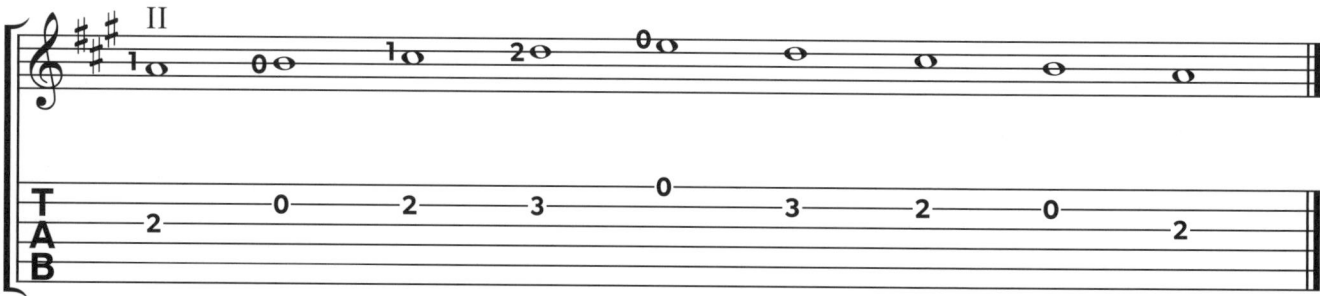

If we play just the first, third and fifth notes of this scale, we get an A major arpeggio.

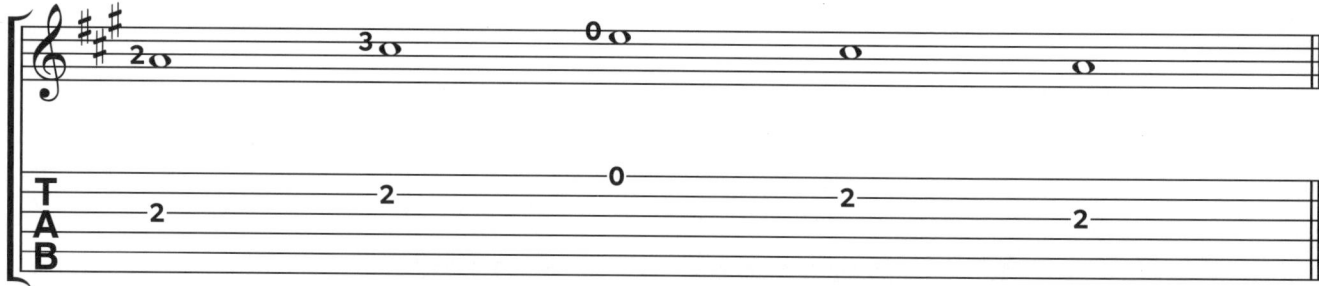

If we play these notes together, we get an A major chord:

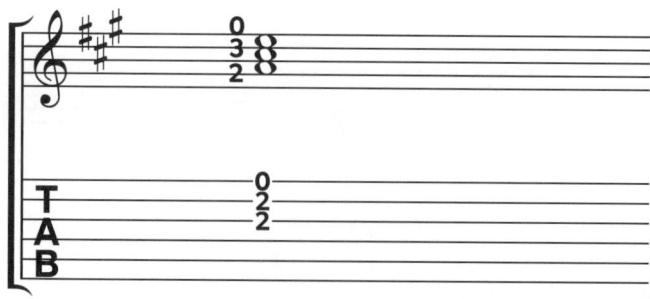

However complex, most music is made of scales, arpeggios and chords combined with rhythms. In the next piece *Allegro*, notice how Mozart uses scales and arpeggios.

ALLEGRO

There is nothing more rewarding than playing music with other people. At the start of my time as a student I have to admit to feeling a little bit lonely. I came from a very different place, and didn't really expect to fit in straight away. However, music has an amazing way of connecting with people.

One of my professors at the Royal Academy of Music, Tim Walker had this crazy idea of arranging a whole Mozart opera for four guitars and three singers! Rehearsing and performing his brilliant, technically demanding arrangement was an amazing experience, and really brought us all together. I remember thinking at the time that it was the most fun I'd ever had!

Mozart himself didn't write a single piece for the guitar, which is a great shame. However, he wrote many duets for wind instruments and many of these work brilliantly for two guitars.

PRO TIP

The thumb is a powerful digit. Nevertheless, in this piece be careful not to make the thumb notes stand out too loudly compared with the other notes. Aim for an even melodic line.

Allegro
No. 8 from *12 Duets*, K 487

10 Audio + PDF of Duet Score

W. A. Mozart
1756-1791
arr. Carl Herring

THE TROUT

from *Die Forelle, D. 550*

When I came to London, I was bowled over by the sheer number of opportunities for hearing great live music. My love of chamber music frequently led me to the Wigmore Hall, arguably the world's finest venue for it. One of the most featured composers in the concerts I heard there was Schubert.

During the course of his short life Schubert composed hundreds of pieces, many of them songs. He was a master of melody and expression. This theme comes from a song Schubert wrote for solo voice and piano. It must have been incredibly popular, as he used the same melody again in one of his most celebrated works, his *Trout Quintet* (*Piano Quintet in A major, D. 667*).

PRO TIP

Like in *Beautiful Moonlight* (page 23), we use the right hand fingers and thumb at the same time. Again, it's a good idea to try both parts separately before putting them together.

The Trout
from *Die Forelle, D. 550*

 11 Audio

Franz Schubert
1797–1828
arr. Martin Hegel

© 2018 Schott Music Ltd., London

DEVELOPING SPEED

One of the most exciting things for me when I just started playing the guitar, was being able to play really fast. As young students, my friends and I used to compete with each other as to who had faster fingers! Practising with a metronome* is a great way to increase velocity.

Play the following exercise several times, each time increasing the tempo by just a notch or two.

Exercise

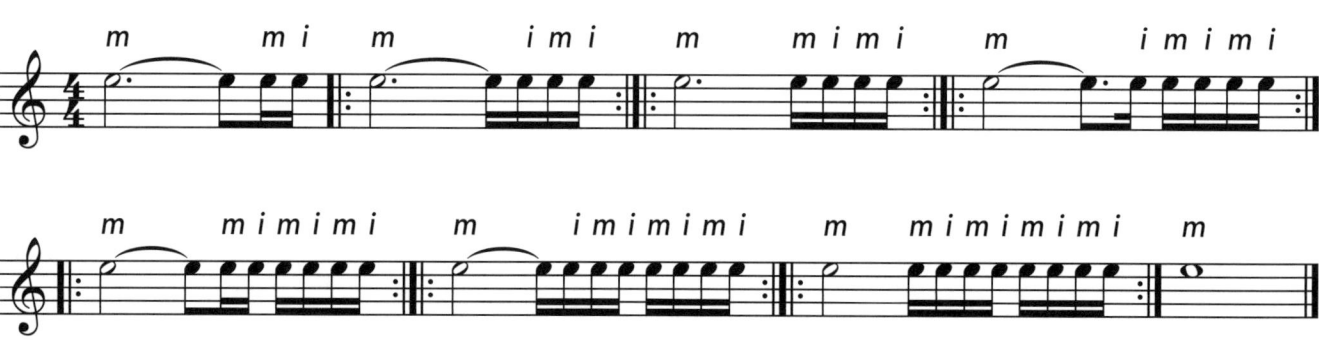

Now try the same exercise starting on **i**.
You could also use **m** and **a**, or **i** and **a**.

Brigands Are Dancing is a fun piece for showing off how fast you can play!
I recommend practising bars 2 and 5 by themselves.

As you did with the exercise above, use a metronome to gradually increase the speed.

PRO TIP

When playing for other people, play slightly slower than your maximum speed.
Having this 'headroom' will mean that as well as being fast, you will also sound like you're in full control.

*Please see page 68 for accessory recommendations.

Brigands Were Dancing
Tancyli Zbójnicy

12 Audio

© 2018 Schott Music Ltd., London

SLURS

A **slur** is a note played with the left hand alone. Looking at the exercise below, you can see that slurs come in two types. The second note of each bar should be played by the left hand alone. Try this with each finger in turn.

Exercise 1

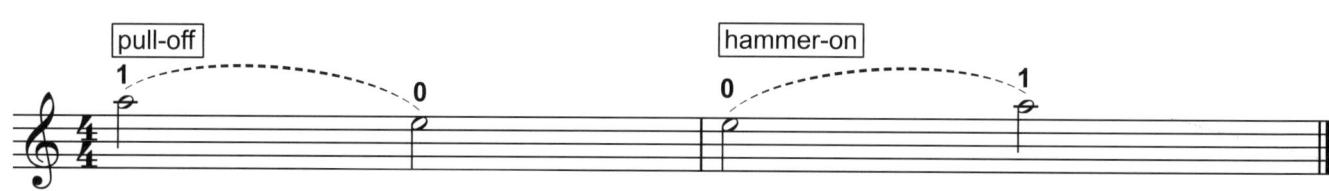

Now try the same thing on different strings and on different parts of the neck.

We can also slur to and from other fretted notes.
For the pull-off, have your finger already fretting the second note before you play the first note.

Exercise 2

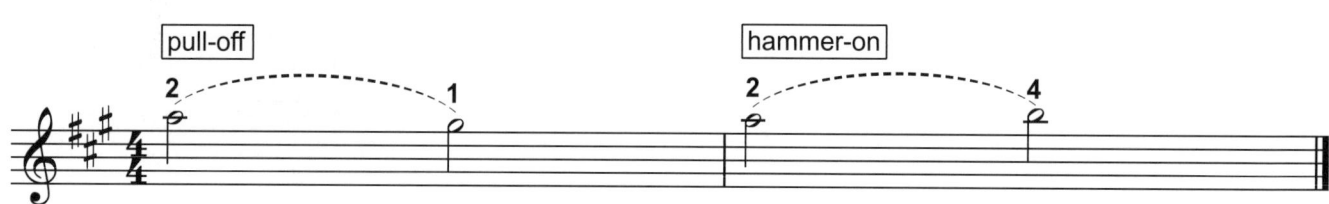

Now try using slurs in bar 5 of *Brigands Were Dancing* as an alternative to striking every note.

Exercise 3

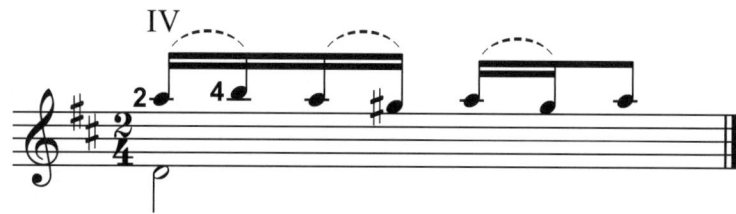

TWO 19TH-CENTURY GUITAR HEROES: SOR & GIULIANI

Fernando Sor and Mauro Giuliani are names that every classical guitarist should know. They were both highly influential and made huge contributions to the repertoire for the guitar.

Fernando Sor (1778-1839)

Known in his native Spain as 'the Beethoven of the guitar', Sor was famous in his lifetime both as a composer and as a virtuoso performer. Before spending the latter part of his life in Paris, he lived in London for several years. He travelled widely, performing in St. Petersburg, Moscow, Berlin and Warsaw.

His etudes are the bread and butter to any serious guitar student, loved not only for their instructional value, but also for their fine musical quality. Over the years I have played so many of his pieces and they are always fun and imaginative.

Mauro Giuliani (1781-1829)

Giuliani enjoyed fame as a virtuoso and gave concerts all over Europe. He lived in Vienna for many years, where he became acquainted with Rossini and Beethoven. In fact, it is thought that he played cello in the first performance of Beethoven's Seventh Symphony in 1813. His guitar pieces are still played by guitarists of all levels of ability.

Leçon
Op. 60, No. 2

13 Audio

[♩ = 125]

Fernando Sor
1778-1839

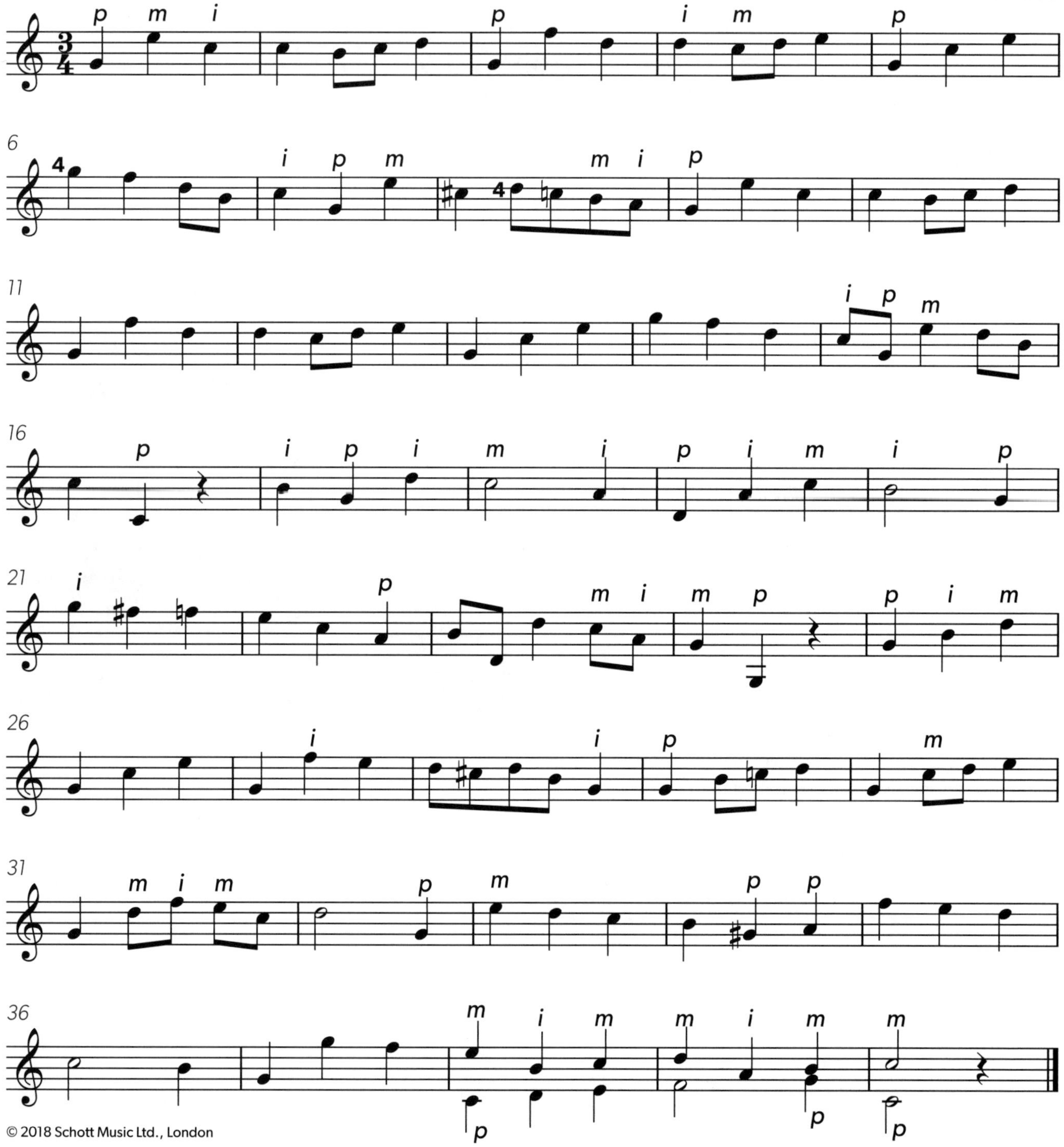

Écossaise in A minor
Op. 33, No. 10

14 Audio

Mauro Giuliani
1781-1829

Fine

D.C. al Fine

© 2018 Schott Music Ltd., London

THE BARRÉ

Sometimes, it's useful to use the same finger to cover more than one string. This is called a barré. Let's try it on strings ① and ② first:

- Notice how I'm pressing slightly with the side of my finger.

- Bringing your elbow in towards your body will help you to get a good, clear sound.

- Press as close to the fret as possible.

Exercise 1

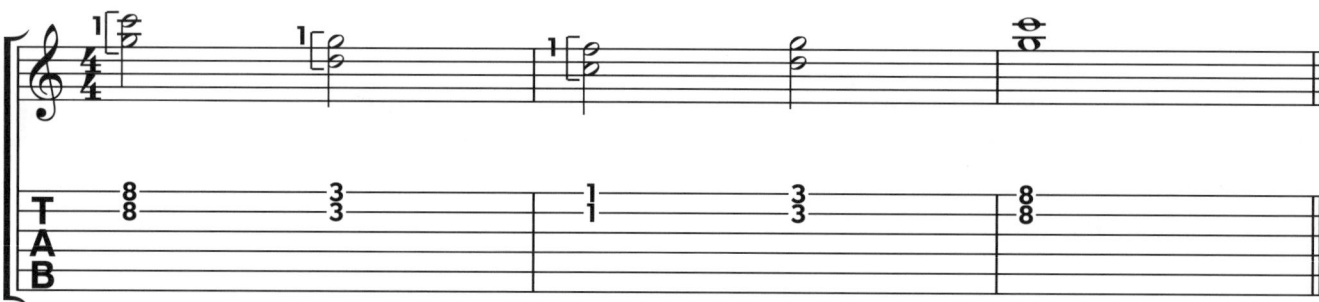

Now let's try a barré in combination with another finger. In the last chord, there is a barré across three strings:

Exercise 2

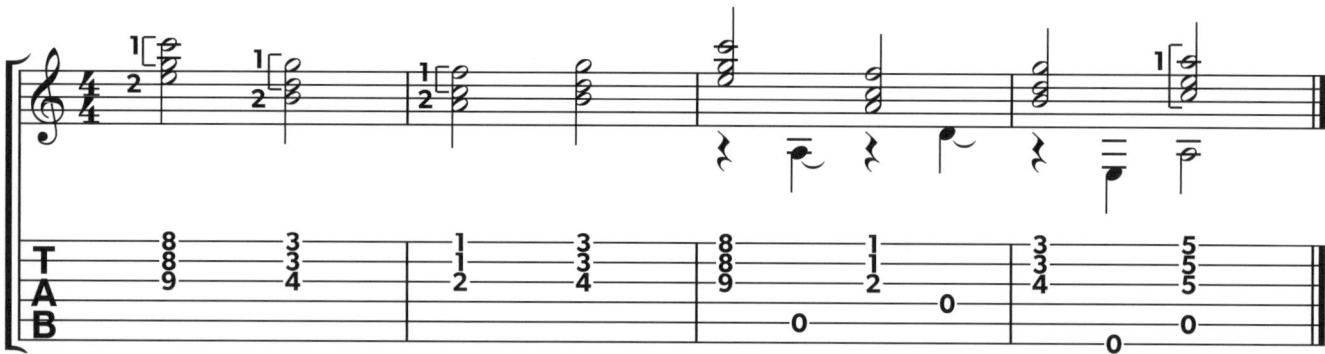

A UNIVERSAL SOUND

While the major scale contains seven different tones, the **pentatonic** scale contains only five. Pentatonic music is believed to have arisen completely independently in many distinct cultures around the world. Perhaps the pentatonic scale is part of everyone's musical core from birth.

Enjoy the natural, timeless sound of the following two pentatonic scales. It also sounds good if you link them together.

C major pentatonic:

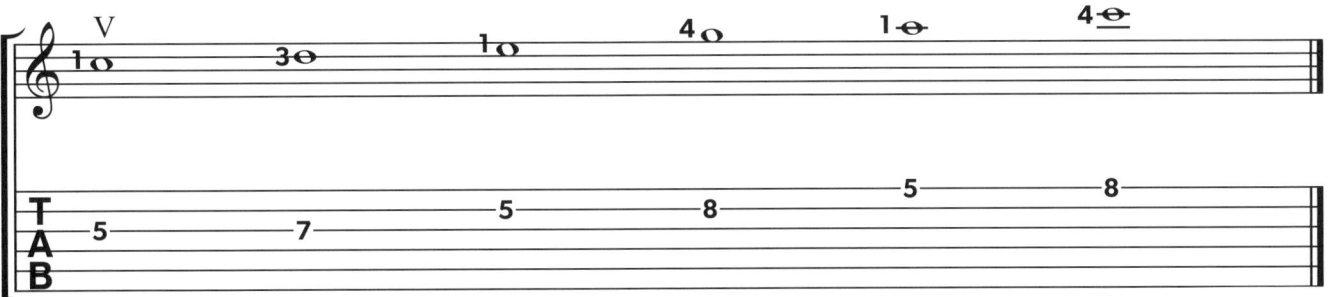

A minor pentatonic:

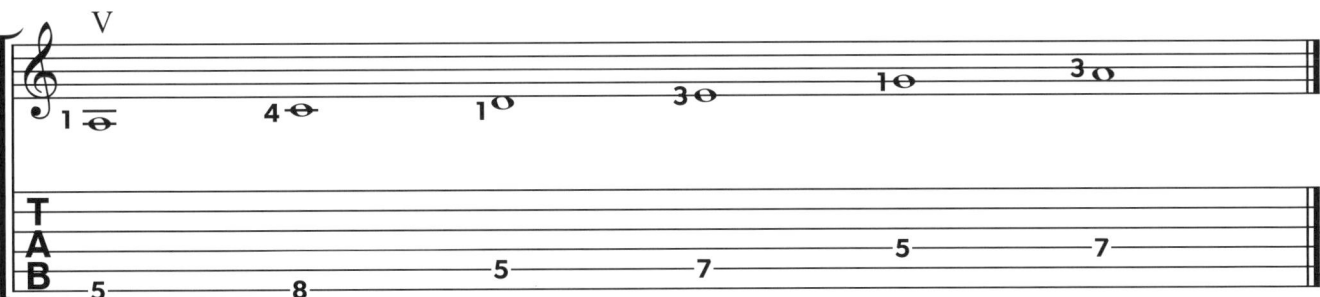

CANTO

from *Guitarcosmos 1*

Canto is a pentatonic piece. It is composed entirely of the tones C, D, E, G and A. In fact, D only appears in the accompaniment and not in the melody at all.

Using Barrés

Canto gives us a great chance to try out our barrés! Using a barré where indicated will avoid the need for finger 1 to jump strings, and will allow you to connect these notes seamlessly. The last two notes of bar 13 and the first note of bar 14 will feel very familiar if you've already played the exercise on page 50. Elsewhere, the barrés are across strings ② and ③ only, meaning you don't really need to apply pressure with the part of your finger covering string ①.

Improvisation

Improvisation is an important part of many musical styles and cultures around the world. It's only relatively recently that it's been neglected by classical musicians. Bach, Beethoven, Mozart and Liszt all used to love improvising! Personally, I had great fun with improvisation when I was working on my Beatles project.

The best way to start is to pick a scale and experiment with playing the notes in different orders and using various rhythmic combinations.

In *Canto*, after you've learned and played the melody that is written, have fun improvising your own melodies along to the same accompaniment. Use the pentatonic scales on page 51.

Canto (Pentatonic Mode)
from *Guitarcosmos 1*

15 Audio + PDF of Duet Score

Reginald Smith Brindle
1917-2003

© 2018 Schott Music Ltd., London

CHORD CORNER 3
A JAZZ 'TURNAROUND'

Often, jazz musicians get to the end of a song, but want to go straight back to the beginning and play it again without a break. In this case, they use a turnaround. This is a chord sequence that creates a smooth link from the end of a piece back to the beginning.

Turnarounds also sound great just on their own, just repeated over and over.

There are many types of turnaround, but this one is by far the most common:

I – VI – ii – V turnaround in C major

16 Audio

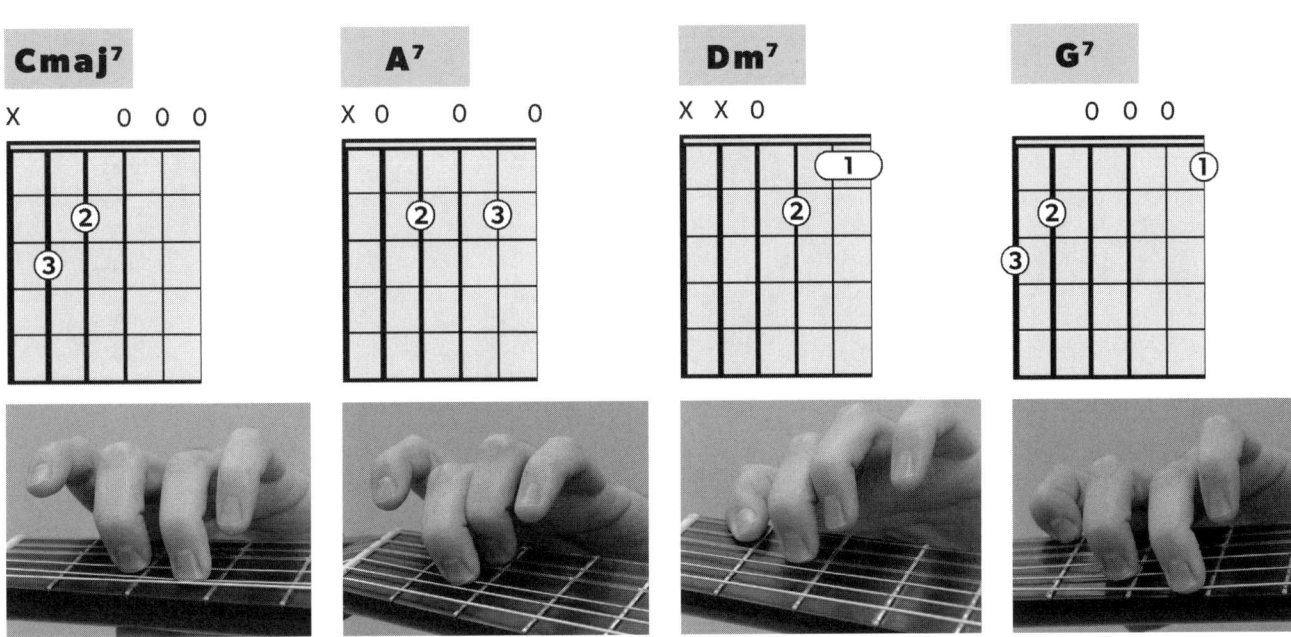

- You'll notice that we played Dm7 in the second of the barré exercises on page 50.

- G7 will feel very familiar from the last two lines of *Aeolian Mode* (page 27). Again, if it's difficult, use a capo.

- Record yourself playing the above progression on loop or have a friend play it. Try using the natural minor / Aeolian mode on page 26 to create solos. Get a feel for which notes sound best over each chord.

MUNDO VIVO

Some of the most exciting and colourful music in the world comes from Brazil. When I first visited Brazil I was incredibly inspired by the mix of cultures and variety of influences in the music I heard there, and by the rhythms in particular.

Seeing people move to this wonderful music is enough to stir up passion in anyone. It made such a great impression on me, that I went on to dedicate a whole recording project, *Latino*, to the music of South America.

Mundo Vivo (Lively World) is a piece which really showcases the Brazilian joy of rhythm. It is much easier to pick up these rhythms by ear than to read them from the score. So be sure to listen to the recording several times. Give yourself a chance to really get a feel for how the melody goes before attempting to play it.

Once you've internalised the rhythm of the melody, you'll see that it's not as difficult as it looks on the page.

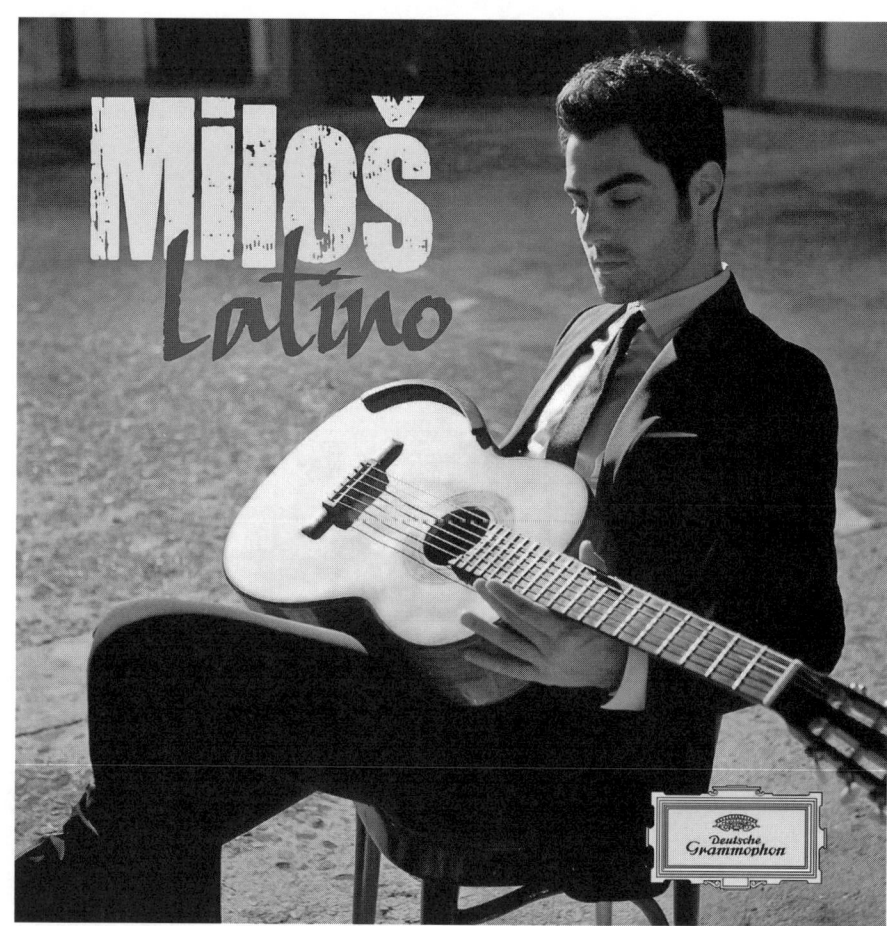

Percussion

The guitar can be a great percussion instrument too, so enjoy playing those taps! (♩). Personally, I tap the edge of the guitar with my fingertips. I like the sound it makes, and it's not a part of the guitar that would be easily damaged if I got carried away!

Mundo Vivo

17 Audio + PDF of Duet Score

John Crawford (1969)
arr. Carl Herring

MENUETT I

If I had to choose one composer to play forever, it would be Bach!

Actually, the guitar as we know it did not yet exist during Bach's lifetime. However, his music is so timeless and beautiful that it really sounds gorgeous on any instrument. Indeed, Bach himself often made new arrangements of his own pieces.

This piece was written for keyboard when Bach was about seventeen. My life changed forever at seventeen when I moved to London and started my studies at the Royal Academy of Music. Bach's music soon became an essential cornerstone of my development as a musician.

When distinct melody lines intertwine and work in harmony, this is called polyphony. Bach's polyphonic writing was so good that it has been studied and admired by every subsequent composer.

Miloš studying Bach

Menuett I
from *BVW 822*

18 Audio + PDF of Duet Score

Johann Sebastian Bach
1685-1750
arr. Carl Herring

© 2018 Schott Music Ltd., London

CHORD CORNER 4

These are the chords I, IV and V in the key of D.

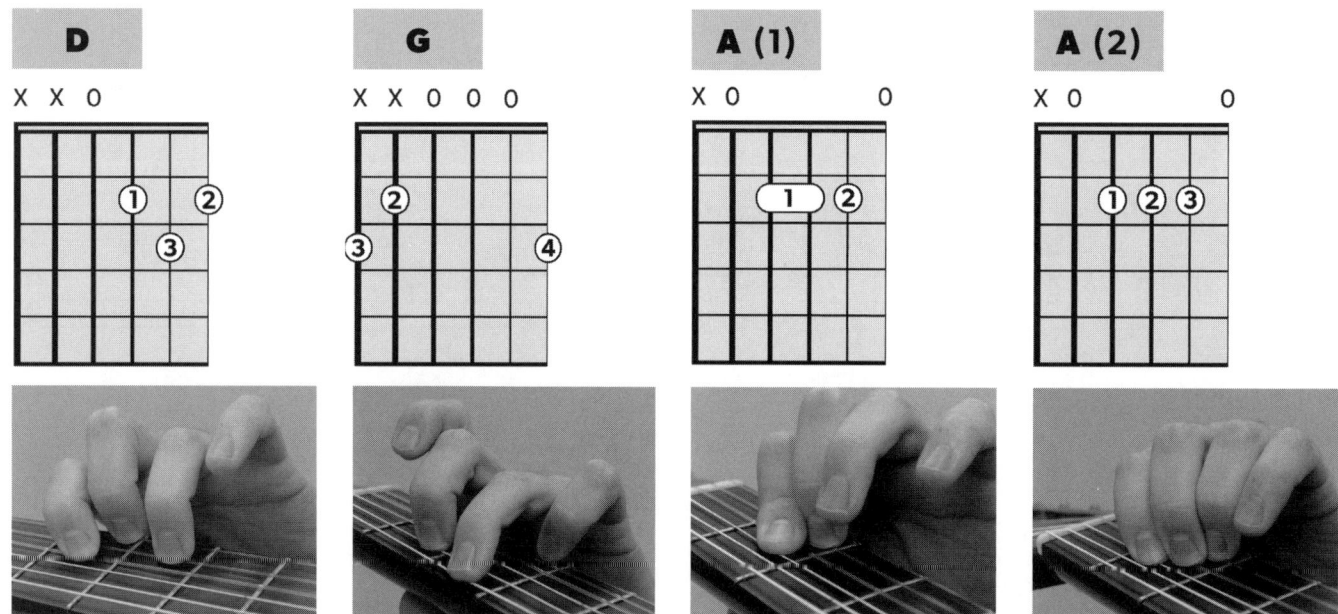

Before we turn our attention to the *Canario* on page 61, let's take a moment to examine its harmonic structure by playing the progression below.

Canario

D	**D**	**D**	**A**	**D**
D	**D**	**D**	**A**	**D**
G A	**D**	**D**	**A**	**D**
G A	**D**	**D**	**A**	**D**

SLURS AND ORNAMENTS

By doing hammer-ons and pull-offs in quick succession, we can create **ornaments**. Here is an exercise that will help you to play the ornaments in *Canario*.

Exercise 1

In this next exercise all the fingers stay pressed down except for finger 2, which does hammer-ons.

Exercise 2

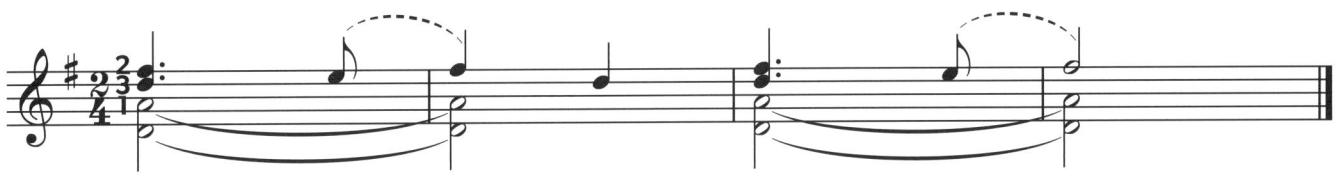

THE BAROQUE GUITAR

If you look at the guitar below, you'll notice that it probably looks quite different from your guitar. It's a Baroque guitar, the kind that the Italian guitarist Carlo Calvi would have played.

As well as being smaller, it had five gut courses (in this case four pairs of strings and one single string). Even though the tuning was a bit different, pieces written for the Baroque guitar usually work very well on the modern guitar too.

Canario

The *canario* was a lively dance which involved a lot of foot tapping. On my album *Aranjuez*, the last movement of *Fantasia Para Un Gentilhombre* is a *canario*. In fact, Rodrigo borrowed this *canario* from the Spanish guitarist Gaspar Sanz (1640-1710). Sanz's is undoubtedly the most famous *canario* in the guitar repertoire, and we'll learn it in book four of this series.

In this piece, notice how your hand makes a D chord shape as you play bars 10-11 and 14-15.

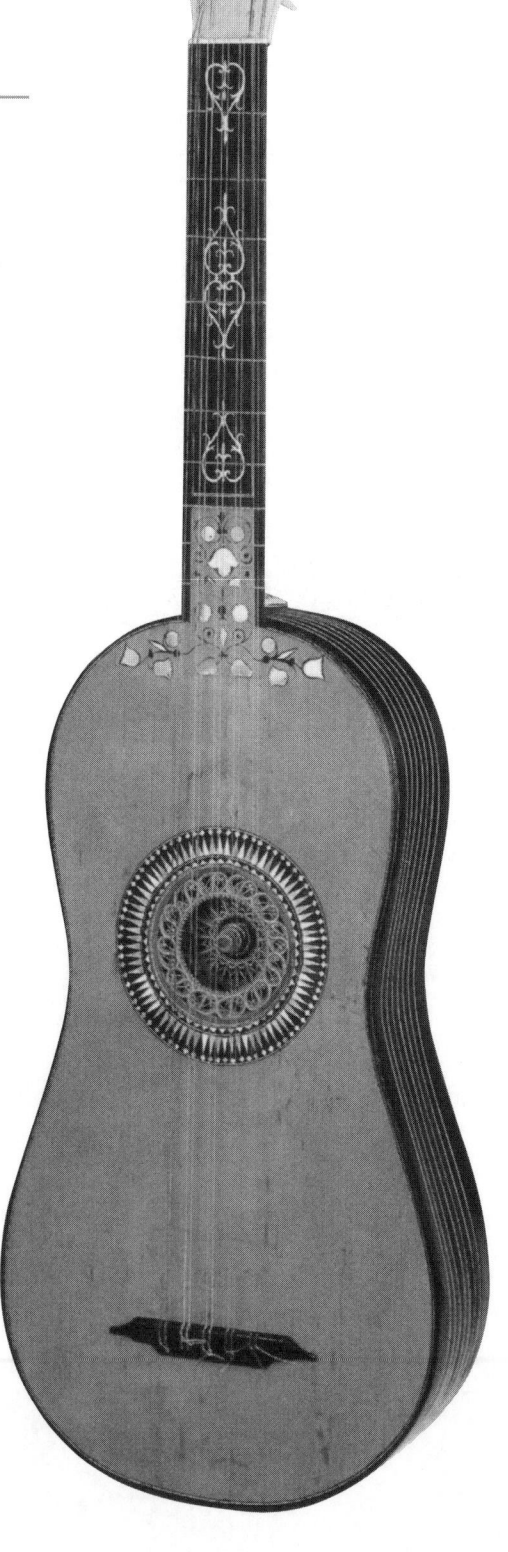

Canario

from *Intavolatura Di Chitarra e Chitarriglia* (Bologna 1646)

Carlo Calvi
1612-1669

PASTIME WITH GOOD COMPANY

This is a song about the joy of having a good time with friends.
The composer of this song, King Henry VIII, clearly knew how to throw a party!
The lyrics to this song begin:

Pastime with good company
I love, and shall until I die

Very often, when I come back from a tour and meet with my close friends,
we would end up singing and playing late into the night.

Pastime with Good Company

20 Audio

Henry VIII King of England
1491 - 1547
arr. Carl Herring

© 2018 Schott Music Ltd., London

HARMONICS

The guitar can make some magical bell-like tones. Produced by a special technique, these notes are called **harmonics**. The easiest place to play them is at the twelfth fret. Place your finger gently onto the string so that it's just touching it. It should be directly over the fret.

Play quite strongly with your right hand, then take your left hand away to let the harmonic ring out clearly. Try this on different strings.

You can also play harmonics in other places, such as over the fifth and seventh frets.

Harmonics are notated with diamond note heads.

The picture here shows how to play the first harmonic in the next piece, *Song of the Seashore*.

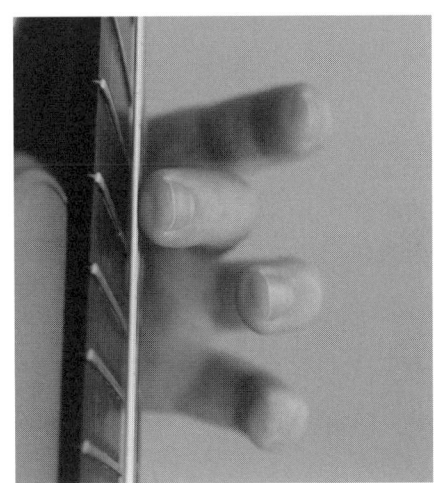

SONG OF THE SEASHORE

(Hamabe no Uta)

I always look forward to performing in Japan. It has amazing concert halls, the most respectful and kind audiences, and food to die for!

My first visit to Japan is something I'll never forget. I had the pleasure of hearing someone play the shakuhachi (a Japanese flute) for me. *Song of the Seashore* is the song they played.

I am told that every Japanese person knows this song. Its lyrics describe the beauty of the seaside and the memories associated with it.

Aim to create a calm, gentle mood. The lilting [6/8] rhythm may suggest to you the lapping of waves on a beach.

To make sure there's no doubt about where to play the harmonics, tablature has been included for this piece.

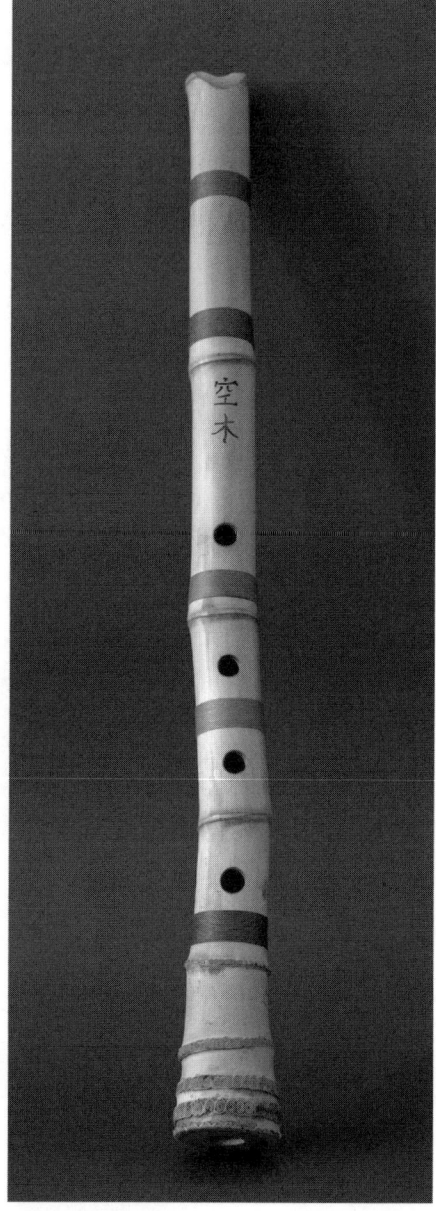

The shakuhachi

Song of the Seashore

浜辺の歌 (Hamabe no Uta)

21 Audio

Tamezo Narita
1893 -1945
arr. Carl Herring

Gently [♩. = 44]

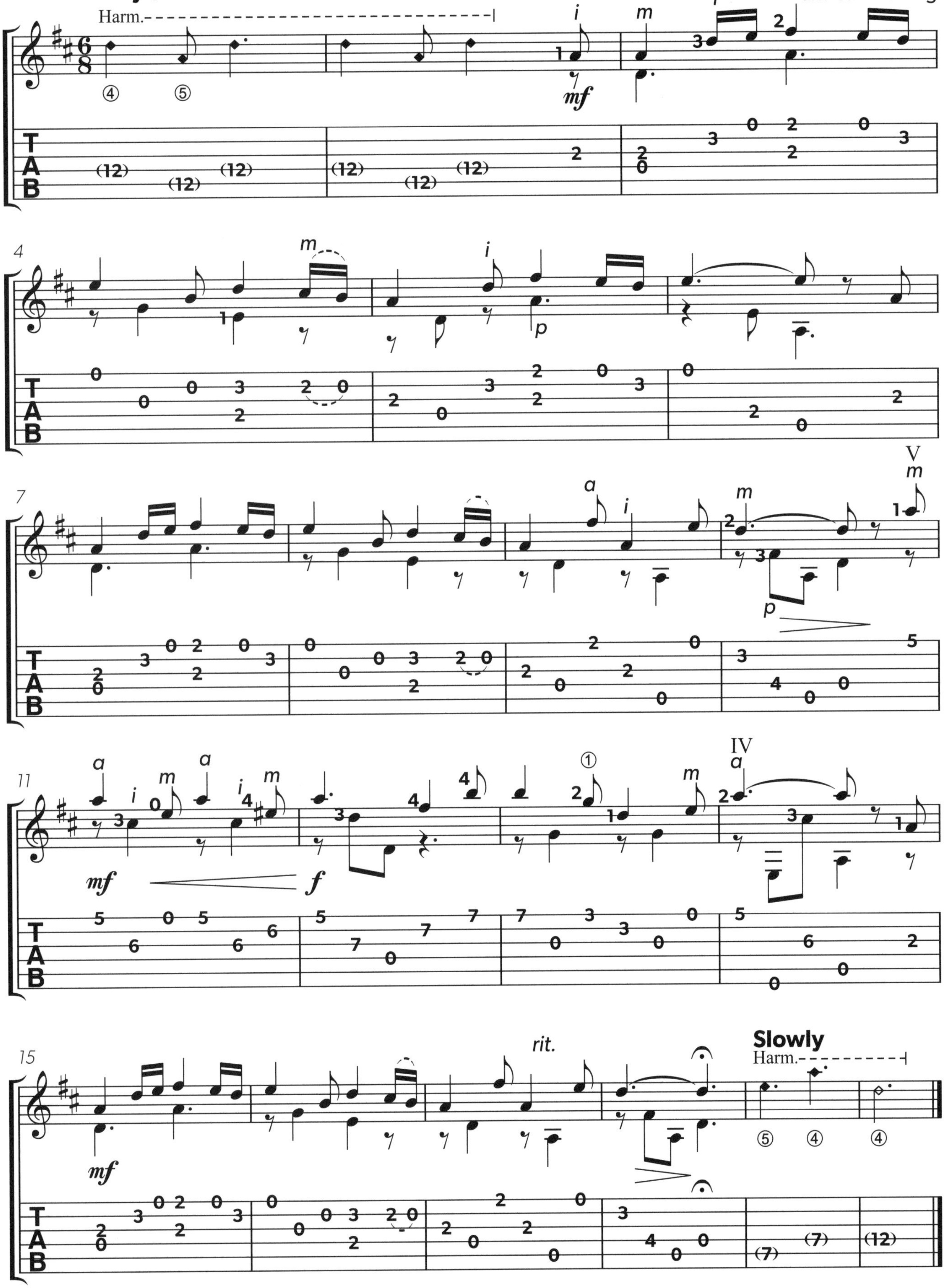

CONGRATULATIONS!

You've now reached the end of Level 1!

Along the way, you've deepened your knowledge of the guitar and have greatly strengthened your technique. The chords you've learned will serve you well, as you notice their familiar shapes appearing time and again in the new pieces that you learn. Most importantly, you've learned some great repertoire!

As you move on to Level 2, be sure to revisit these familiar pieces frequently. You'll notice that they'll seem easier and easier, but keep playing them, and you might discover things that you hadn't noticed before.

Remember too that good music doesn't have to be technically challenging! Many of the pieces I enjoy playing most are actually not technically demanding.

I'm really looking forward to seeing you in Level 2. We're going to build on what you've learned here as we cover more techniques, chords, theory, tips and pieces.

As with this book, you'll find a wealth of content that is unavailable elsewhere.

See you very soon,

Available from all good music shops or direct from www.playguitarwithmilos.com

DISCOGRAPHY

2011

Mediterráneo   DG Deutsche Grammophon

2012

Latino   DG Deutsche Grammophon

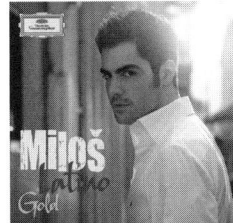

2012

Latino Gold   DG Deutsche Grammophon

2014

Aranjuez   DG Deutsche Grammophon

2016

Blackbird: The Beatles Album   Decca/Mercury Classics

RECOMMENDED ACCESSORIES

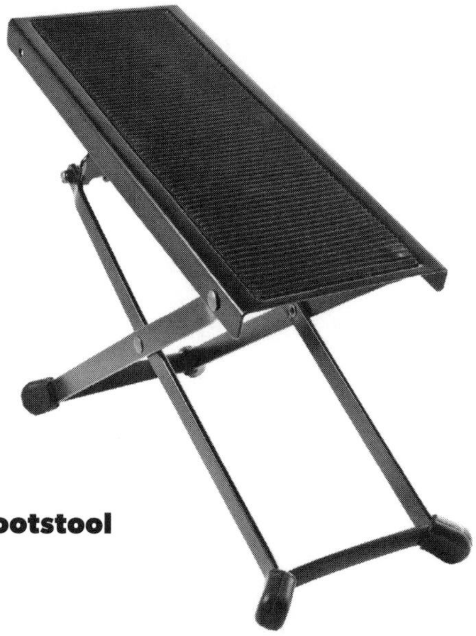

footstool

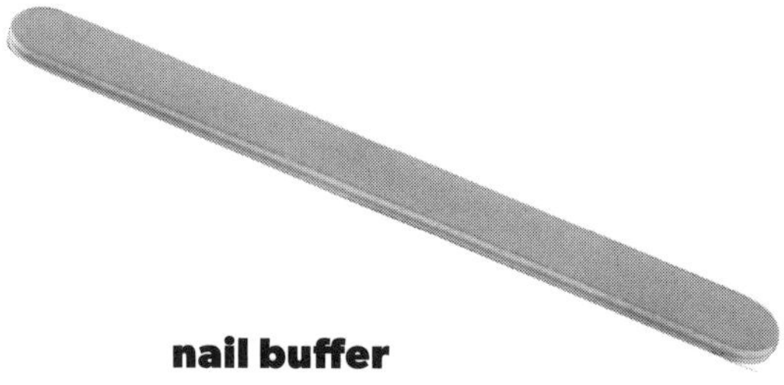

nail buffer

music stand

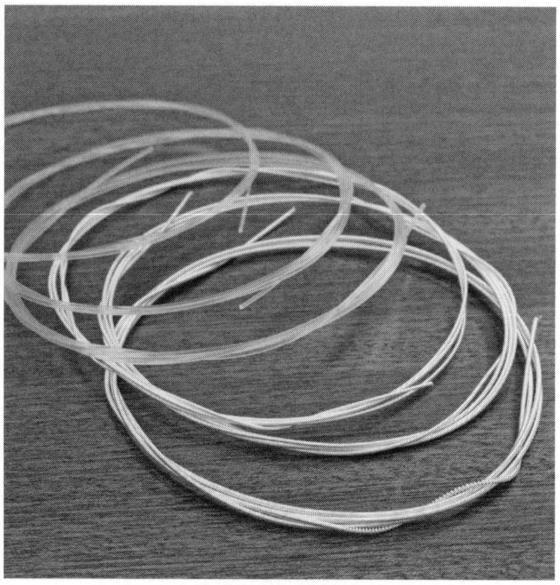

strings

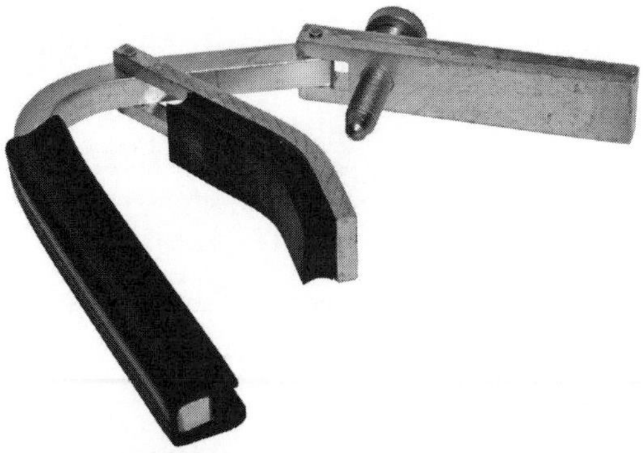

capo

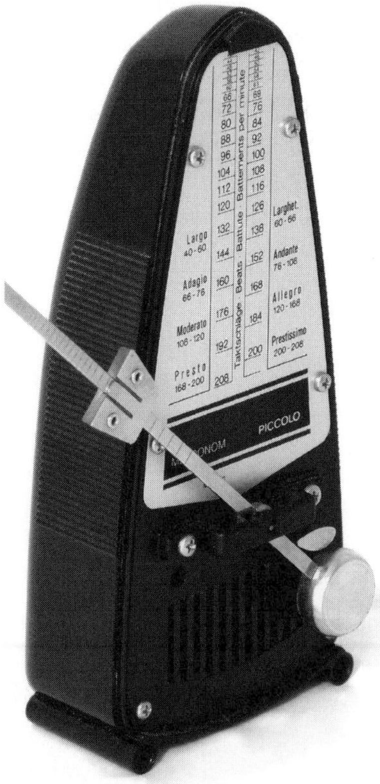

metronome

GLOSSARY

In the world of guitar music, terms relating to technique are usually in Spanish (Sp.) or English. Wider musical terms are generally in Italian (It.), although French (Fr.) and German are not uncommon.

①	string 1
a (anular) (Sp.)	ring ringer of the plucking hand
adagio (It.)	slowly
Aeolian mode	see *natural minor scale*
allegro (It.)	quickly, brightly
andante (It.)	at a walking pace
andante con moto (It.)	slightly faster than walking pace; *con moto* = 'with motion'
apoyando (Sp.)	see *rest stroke*
arpeggio (It.)	the notes of a chord played one after the other in an ascending and/or descending order
a tempo (It.)	resume the previous *tempo*
Baroque (Fr.)	the musical period between approximately 1600 and 1750
barré (Fr.)	using a single finger to press down multiple strings
canario (It.), (Sp.)	a dance popular all over Europe in the late 16th and early 17th centuries
capo (capotasto) (It.)	a clamp-like device which effectively creates a new nut higher than the guitar's actual nut; literally 'head of the fretboard'
coda (It.)	the final section of a piece, literally 'tail'
crescendo (It.)	(⟨) a gradual increase in loudness
decrescendo (It.)	(⟩) a gradual decrease in loudness
dolce (It.)	sweetly
D.S. al Fine (It.)	Repeat from the sign 𝄋 and continue until the word *Fine*.
écossaise (Fr.)	a Scottish-style country dance, usually in 2/4 time; literally 'Scottish'
f, forte (It.)	loudly
fifth position (V)	This refers to the location of the hand on the fretboard. In fifth position, fingers 1-4 are assigned notes at frets 5, 6, 7 and 8 respectively.
ff, fortissimo (It.)	very loudly
fine (It.)	the end
free stroke	Unlike in the rest stroke, the finger does not rest on an adjacent string after striking a string. also called tirando
hammer-on	playing a note with a fretting-hand finger only by bringing it down quickly onto the fretboard
harmonic	a special kind of note with a bell-like quality
i (indice) (Sp.)	index finger of the plucking hand
legato (It.)	connect the notes smoothly
m (medio) (Sp.)	middle finger of the plucking hand
mf, mezzo-forte (It.)	moderately loudly

mode	scales based on various different sequences of tones and semitones	round	a piece for several players who play the same music but starting one after the other
moderato (It.)	at a moderate tempo		
mp, mezzo-piano (It.)	moderately quietly	scale	notes arranged in stepwise ascending and/or descending order
natural sign ♮	indicates that the note it is place before is not a sharp (♯) or flat (♭)	slur	1. a curved line indicating that notes are to be played without separation;
natural minor scale	The scale consisting of the same series of whole and half steps as the natural diatonic scale A-A. Also called the *Aeolian mode*.		2. a 'technical' slur covering both hammer-ons and pull-offs
ornament	notes of decoration	staccato (It.)	play the notes in a short, detached, unconnected way
pentatonic	music based on five notes, usually lacking semitones	tempo (It.)	the speed of the music
p	quietly	timbre (Fr.)	a particular quality of tone
p (pulgar) (Sp.)	thumb of the plucking hand	turnaround	in jazz, a passage or series of chords at the end of a piece that lead back to the beginning
plant	prepare the fingers on the strings		
poco (It.)	slightly, a little	V (chord five) cf. **I**, **ii**, **IV**, etc.	a chord built on the fifth step of a scale
pull-off	playing a note with a fretting-hand finger only by		
pulse	the music's regular beat		
position	The location of the hand on the fretboard.		
pp, pianissimo (It.)	very quietly		
progression	a repeating series of chords		
rall. (rallentando) (It.)	gradually slowing down		
rest stroke	After striking the string, the finger rests on the adjacent string. Also called *apoyando*		
rit. (ritenuto) (It.)	'held back', immediately slowing down		

Upper case Roman numerals refer to major chords, while lower case Roman numerals are used for minor chords.

HOW TO READ TABLATURE (TAB)

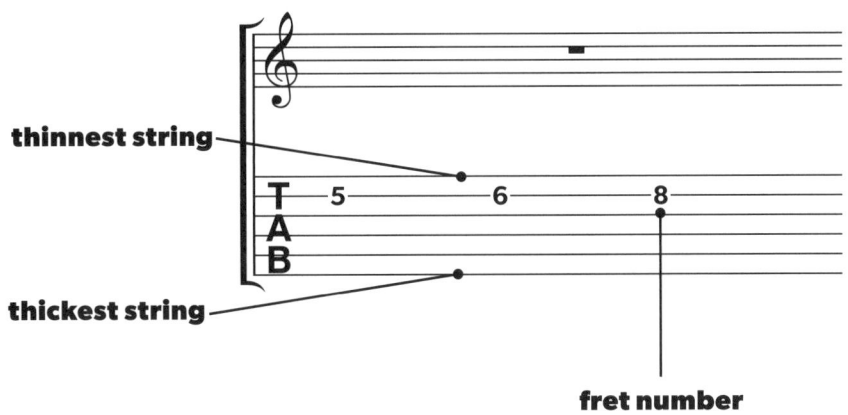

So, the notes above would be found here:

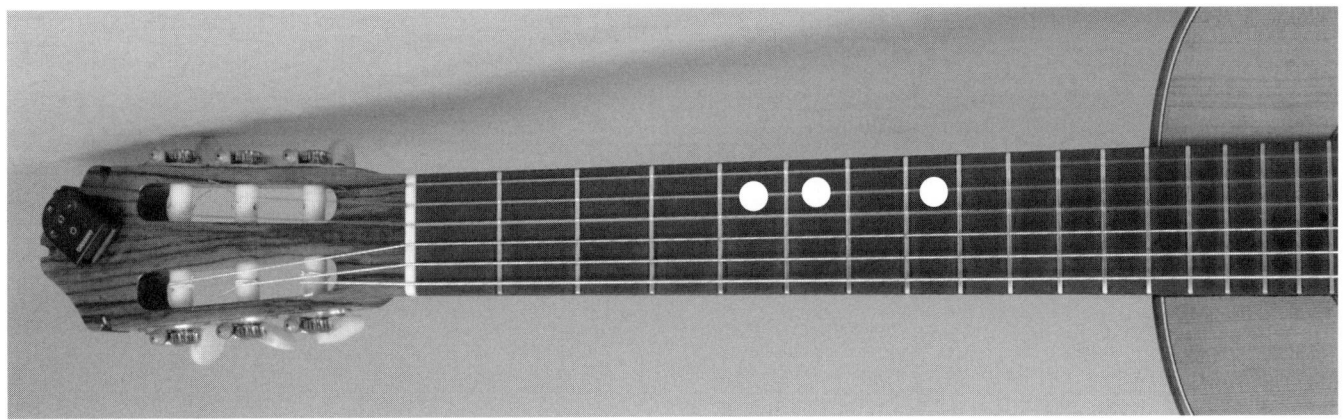

The **G chord** introduced on page 22 would look this this if written in tablature:

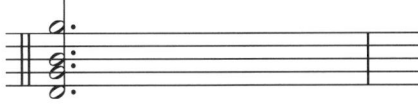

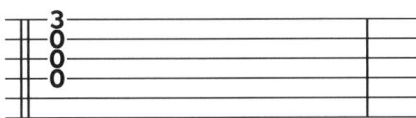

Note that:

- Open strings are indicated by zeros.
- Stacked numbers are notes played at the same time.

FRETBOARD MAP

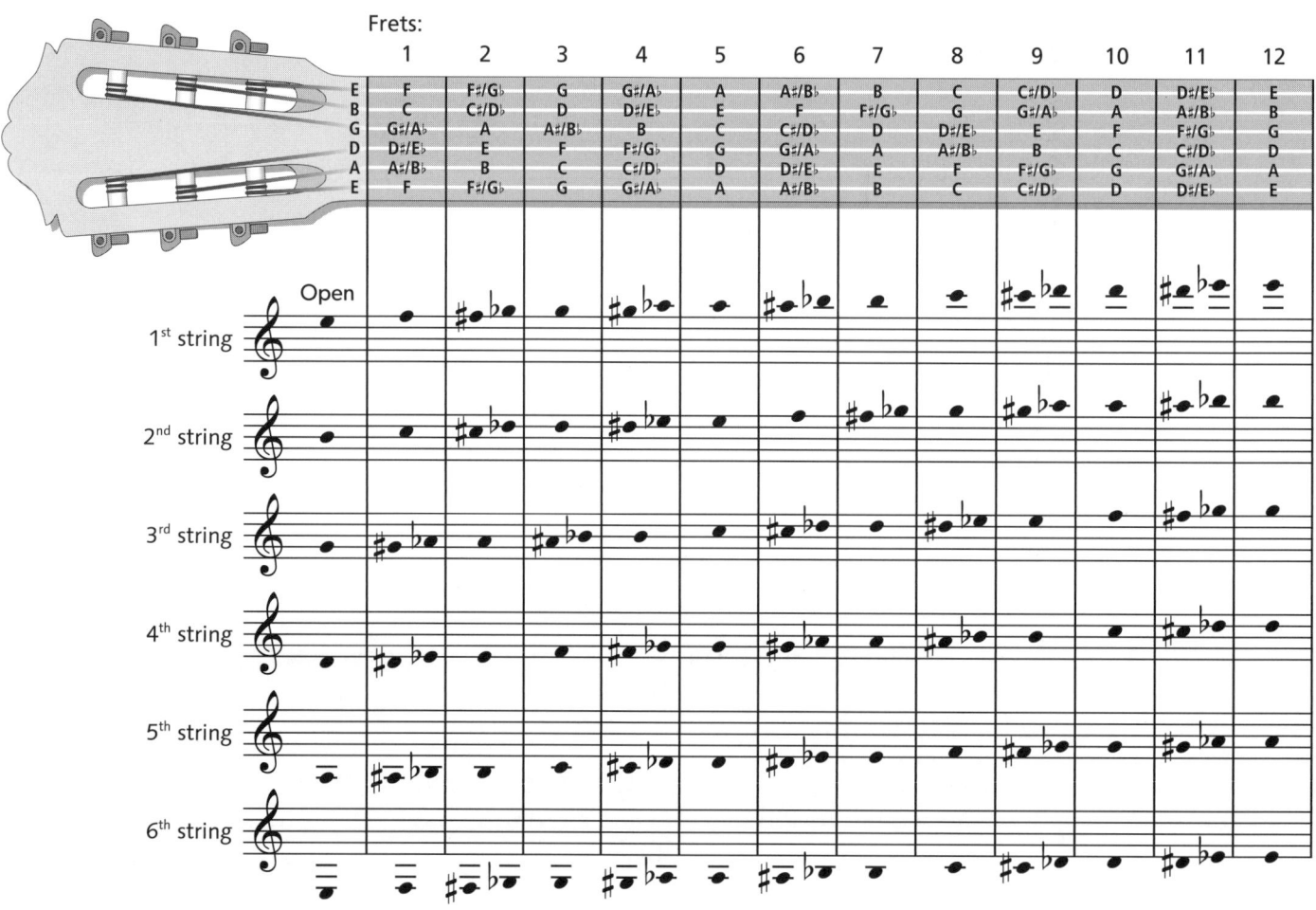